THE
GOOMBA
DIET

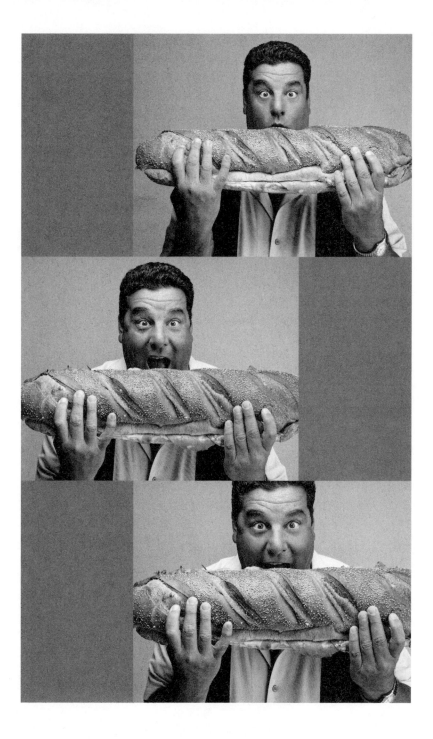

A Goomba's Guide to Life

The Goomba's Book of Love

Nicky Deuce: Welcome to the Family

THE GOOMBA DIET

Living Large and Loving It

STEVEN R. SCHIRRIPA

AND CHARLES FLEMING

CLARKSON POTTER/PUBLISHERS
NEW YORK

Published in the United States by Clarkson Potter/Publishers, an imprint of the
Crown Publishing Group, a division of Random House, Inc., New York.
www.crownpublishing.com
www.clarksonpotter.com

Clarkson N. Potter is a trademark and Potter and colophon
are registered trademarks of Random House, Inc.

Library of Congress Cataloging-in-Publication Data

Schirripa, Steven R.
The goomba diet : living large and loving it / Steven R. Schirripa
and Charles Fleming.—1st ed.
1. Italian Americans—Humor. 2. Diet—Humor. I. Fleming, Charles. II. Title.
PN6231.I85S32   2006
818.602—dc22   2005037247

ISBN 13: 978-1-4000-5463-3
ISBN 10: 1-4000-5463-X

Printed in the United States of America

Design by Maggie Hinders

10   9   8   7   6   5   4   3   2   1

First Edition

To the loves of my life,

Laura, Bria, Ciara, and Bobby and Carly.

Acknowledgments

STEVE SCHIRRIPA would like to thank, for their invaluable help in making this book possible, Alexandria Addams, Kip Addotta, Diego Aldana, Frank Anobile Sr., Frank Anobile Jr., Mike Anobile Sr., Mike Anobile Jr., the Anobile family, Ted Arneault, Mario Batali, Valerie Baugh, Tobe Becker, Erin Bix, Pat Bolino, Lorraine Bracco, Tom Burke, Vito Cap, John Capotorto, David Chalfy, David Chase, Dominic Chianese, Diane Costello, Vince Curatola, Michael De Georgio, Carmine Esposito Sr., Edie Falco, Ray Favero, Bob Fiandra, the Fiandra family, Hugh Fink, Aliza Fogelson, Robert Funaro, James Gandolfini, Joseph R. Gannascoli, Laurie Gomez, Roger Haber, Michael Imperioli, Richie and Anthony Iocolano, Pam Krauss, Ilene Landress, Don Learned, Joe Mack, John Manfrellotti, Joe Marzella, John Mascali, Guido Maurino, Johnnyboy Mazzone, Richie McElory, Cheryl McLean, Vinnie Montalto, Charles Najjar, Judge Nancy Oesterle, Lisa Perkins, Johnny Planco, Cecile Cross-Plummer, the Raya family, Geary Rindells, Richard Scanlon, Lorraine Schirripa and the Schirripa family, Jeff Singer, Tony Sirico, Michael Strahan, Angela Tarantino, Teddy D., Steven Van Zandt, John Ventimiglia, David Vigliano, Terry Winter, Barb Wolf, Il Cortile Restaurant, the entire cast and crew of *The Sopranos,* all his friends back in Bensonhurst, his wife Laura and daughters Ciara and Bria, and everyone who helped (you know who you are). The authors would also like to thank Nick Di Paolo and Joe Medeiros.

CHARLES FLEMING wishes to thank Pam Krauss, Aliza Fogelson, David Vigliano, and Gary Morris for making this book possible, and Karl Fleming and Anne Taylor Fleming for teaching him how to cook and how to eat.

Contents

Introduction

Buon giórno and *buon appetito*, everybody! Welcome to the Goomba Diet—the only diet ever designed to help you not lose weight.

You heard me right. This is the Goomba Diet.

We're not talking South Beach or Scarsdale here. This ain't about cutting carbs or counting calories. It's not about losing pounds or inches. It's not about weighing less, or even eating less.

It's about eating more—eating more food, eating better food, eating more often, and having more fun doing it.

Exhibit A? The goomba himself.

The goomba lives big. Everything he does, he does big. He's a little louder, a little friendlier, and a little *hungrier* than everyone else. He's usually a little larger—or a lot larger—inside and out. He's got a big mouth, a big temper, and a big heart, and he doesn't try to hide it. He'll laugh faster, fight faster, and forgive and forget faster than the average guy.

In other words, he's got a big appetite. When he eats, he eats a lot. If he's going out for dinner with friends, he's going to start with a little prosciutto and mozzarella or provolone, or maybe some fried calamari and baked clams, followed by maybe a little minestrone, and after that some shrimp oreganata, then maybe a nice rigatoni à la vodka.

Then he's going to have dinner—chicken parmigiana, veal milanese, or maybe a steak. If it's a big evening, he might order all three of those. With a little escarole, or broccoli rabe. And wine. And an espresso afterward, and a Sambuca, and some cannoli, or a nice ricotta cheesecake. If the restaurant is a long way from where he lives, maybe he stopped for a slice on the way. Maybe he stops for a slice on the way home, too.

Overeaters Anonymous? This is more like Overeaters Unanimous! Everybody I know has a big appetite. It's the goomba way.

But this book isn't just about food. The goomba does not live on bread alone. The goomba has a big appetite for everything he does. He jumps in with both feet. If he's going to have kids, he's going to have more than one. If he's going to have a girlfriend, he's going to have several. If he's buying a car, or a suit or a pair of shoes, he's buying the best. If he's going out for dinner with friends, it's a lot of friends. (The goomba doesn't go anywhere alone.) If he's taking care of his friends, and he's got money, he's taking care of *everybody*. He's going to tip the valet, the doorman, the maître d', the waiter, the wine steward, and the captain. He's going to expect nothing but the best—because he's paying for it in advance.

So this book is designed to help you do everything more—laugh more, love more, work more, play more, and *live* more.

Don't get the wrong idea. This isn't about being a glutton. It's about doing things *right*. Not for nothing, but you go too far with anything and you're a pig.

When I'm talking about the Goomba Diet, I'm talking about the guy who goes out to a restaurant every Saturday night with his friends and his family and has a six-course meal, with coffee and

dessert—and never thinks twice about what it costs or how many calories it involves.

I'm not talking about the guy who eats a gallon of ice cream every night sitting alone in his apartment. That's disgusting. It's like the difference between eating a steak and eating a cow.

I'm talking about the hard-working guy who takes one vacation every five years and does it right. Nothing is too good for him and his wife. He goes to Atlantic City or Las Vegas, takes in a couple of shows, eats in the best restaurants, drinks the best wine, gets the full treatment at the spa, and throws away a couple of bucks at the tables.

I'm not talking about the guy who goes to Florida twice a year, flies down his wife and his *goomar,* and still tries to pick up broads by the pool. That's too much.

I'm talking about the guy who, when he meets a girl that turns him on, tells her so right away. "You got a little Italian in you? You want some?" He knows what he wants and he's not ashamed to ask for it.

I'm not talking about the guy who flies down to the Dominican Republic on one of those sex tours and goes to bed with three different broads every day. At least I'm pretty sure I'm not talking about that guy. Lemme get back to you on that one.

Maybe you're asking, "Why would I want to look like a goomba in the first place?" Maybe you're asking, "What is a goomba, anyway?"

Let's review.

The goomba is a guy from the neighborhood. He's a guy who grew up hanging out on the corner, by the candy store. He's a blue-collar guy with a lot of street smarts. He may not have a university degree, but he thinks fast on his feet. Ask him to work out the "vig" on a guy who's carrying two large, or the payout on a $20 trifecta at Aqueduct, or the likely sentence on a guy who's been up twice on aggravated assault and just got tagged with a third beef, and watch him work. He'll figure the numbers while your average mortgage broker, math whiz, or public defender is still getting his pencil out.

So if he's carrying a little extra weight, it isn't because he doesn't know how to read the scale or add up the calories. It's because he's got different priorities. He's not eating too much because he can't stop. He's eating too much because he likes it.

The trouble is, being a goomba, and having a big appetite for life, he's likely to get carried away. When he eats, he might eat too much. How can he know? Here are some warning signs:

YOU MIGHT BE OVEREATING IF . . .

- When you leave the buffet table, they put crime scene tape around it.
- You ask the waiter for a doggie bag . . . for food off someone else's table.
- Women start asking you if your breasts are real.
- When you leave the smorgasbord, they put an OUT OF BUSINESS sign on it.
- Your grandmother keeps your dinner warm for you—in the bathtub.
- Your Uncle Angie won't let you use his hammock anymore. Or his Barcalounger. Or his toilet.

Most of the goombas I know take their appetite with them wherever they go. Most of them are working guys, and they work as hard as they eat. They show up, do the best they can, and go home. If they're in, they're all the way in—whether they're working the docks, driving a heap, or walking the beat. Or even if they're on TV.

I just finished shooting the sixth season of *The Sopranos*. It's one of the most successful TV series in the history of TV, and it's been the best working experience of my entire life. I *love* it. I've had more fun, and made closer friends, than any time since I was a kid. And I've been very well paid to do it.

But my life hasn't changed at all in any way that matters. I drive a little nicer car. I live in a little nicer house. But I'm still married to the woman I arrived with. I'm still the father of my two daughters. I still have all the friends I had when I first got on the how. I still wear the same clothes, eat the same food, drink the same wine, and go to the same places I went to before I ever heard the name Bobby "Bacala" Baccalieri.

This is who I am. This is not an act: What you see is exactly what you get. I mean, I might goomba it up a little—when I was doing *Hollywood Squares,* or when I'm doing a bit on *The Tonight Show*—but it's still me. If this is not what you want, that's too bad. This is all I got.

I'm still a goomba. Most of the guys I'm friends with—same thing. They're not gangsters or goodfellas. They're not wise guys, or

Who knew Great Whites loved fat goombas?

knockaround guys, even though we all know some. They're just guys from the block who appreciate the finer things in life.

This is the book for every goomba and everybody who wants to live like a goomba. In these pages you're gonna find ideas on how to eat like a goomba, exercise like a goomba, order in restaurants like a goomba, and celebrate with friends like a goomba. There's instructions on how to maintain the Goomba Diet on the holidays, at weddings and funerals, while dating, when you're working, and when you're knocking around.

It's not for everybody. I've traveled around the country. I've seen these double-wide rednecks who are getting the supersize meal at McDonald's three times a day for years at a time. Is that living? I got nothing to say to them.

This book is for the goomba who's eating everything in sight because it tastes so good, and because everywhere he goes in his goomba world people are serving food. No matter if it's morning, noon, or night—or in between, for that matter—the goombas are celebrating with food.

So, first off, let's separate the goombas from the non-goombas.

YOU ARE NOT A GOOMBA IF YOU HAVE EVER SAID . . .

- "Fo-*shizzle.*"
- "Where's the Ragú?"
- "But, that would be stealing."
- "Nothing for me. I just ate."
- "Oy!"
- "That's *fabulous.*"
- "Another Cosmopolitan, please."

Does any of that sound like you? If so, stop reading now. This is the wrong book.

Otherwise, keep going.

Being a goomba has been pretty good to me. For example: A little while ago a bunch of us guys from *The Sopranos* did this charity thing for the Rock and Roll Hall of Fame. It was me and Jim Gandolfini, appearing as Tony Soprano, and Stevie Van Zandt, appearing as Silvio Dante, like on the show. Stevie was going to walk out on stage, with me and Jim acting like his bodyguards, and we were going to present an award. In the audience, there's Bono and U2, and Mariah Carey, and Neil Young. Lou Reed! Chrissie Hynde! *Percy Sledge!* Before we went on, this makeup person started to put powder on my face. I said, "For what? To go on stage? This is what I look like. It is what it is."

I guess it worked out. After the ceremony I was waiting outside for my car. A black Suburban pulls up and who gets out? Bruce Springsteen. He takes one look at me and said, "Hey! Here's the man!" Then he introduces me to his wife, Patti. I'm thinking, "This guy knows who I am?" I guess I didn't need the makeup.

Some of the guys on the show are funny about that. I was on the set last season and I ran into one of the actors on the show. He was in the makeup trailer. I said, "I didn't know you were working today."

"I'm not," he said. "But I got this party tonight, and I want to look good. There'll probably be people taking pictures."

At that exact moment, the makeup person was curling his eyelashes. This guy who plays a Mafia hit man was having someone curl his eyelashes, so he could go to a party.

Not me. I'm the same guy that got here six seasons ago. I could look different, but why? I've come a long way on just being myself. Looking like this is what got me here. You think I should be thinner? So I could work more? Not for nothing, but go downtown. There's a lot of skinny actors in black turtlenecks down there, tending bar and complaining.

This fat goomba from Brooklyn is doing all right.

That's what this book is about. It's a celebration of all the things that make life worth living—family, friends, work, love, and food.

So sit back, read—or just look at the pictures—and enjoy.

CHAPTER 1

The Staff of Life

There's almost nothing in the world a real goomba likes better than eating. Even the goombas who aren't fat. The whole goomba world revolves around food. Family is all about food. Business is done over food. Deals are made at restaurants. Every big social event—from the christening to the wedding to the funeral—is built around the food. The most important question in a goomba's life is not "Do you take this woman to be your lawfully wedded wife?" or "How do you plead?" The most important question in a goomba's life is "When do we eat?"

You can identify the goomba by what he eats, when he eats, how he eats, and how often he eats. In my first book I told you that you might be a goomba if you've ever eaten a sandwich on the toilet. If that sounds like you, you might already be on the Goomba Diet without even knowing it. If you're not sure, here are some more clues:

YOU ARE ON THE GOOMBA DIET IF . . .
- The air freshener in your car is a slice of provolone.
- Your idea of "health food" is vegetable lasagna.
- Your second word as a baby, after "Mamma," was "mozz-a-rella."

The goomba is a hungry man. He needs to eat often and in large portions. And he's particular about what he eats. He's not interested in exotic foods or exotic animals. Don't tempt him with anything made out of raccoon or rattlesnake.

He wants a regular meal, served in a regular way. He's happy to eat a turkey dinner, but don't try to feed him any turkey burgers, turkey sausages, or any of that other fake diet food. Don't bring him any beefalo. Don't bring him any Spam. Don't even think about tofu burgers or Tofutti ice cream.

He'll order out for Chinese, but that's about it for foreign food. You're wasting your time if you think you're going to get him into that little Indonesian place in SoHo, or the quaint Moroccan hideaway in the Village. He'll eat in a diner owned by a Greek guy, but he's not going to order the stuffed grape leaves. Here's another partial list of the stuff the goomba's not going to eat.

YOU'LL NEVER SEE A GOOMBA EAT . . .
- Grits.
- Gruyère cheese.
- Frog's legs.
- Any other part of the frog.
- Any weird animal that "tastes like chicken." If the goomba wants to eat something that tastes like chicken, he's going to order the chicken.
- Anything macrobiotic. Or microbiotic.

Bottom line, the goomba ain't missing too many meals. How can you tell? Look at the guy. Most goombas are pretty big. They don't look hungry. They don't look like they've ever been on a diet in their whole lives.

If this doesn't sound like you, or anybody you know, you might not be a goomba at all. But you might still need the Goomba Diet.

YOU NEED THE GOOMBA DIET IF . . .
- You have an offensive nickname, like Joey the Stomach.
- Your waist size is larger than your IQ.
- It's been more than a month since you saw your penis.
- They start asking you to use the freight elevator at your apartment.
- It takes more than two people holding hands to give you the Heimlich.

Food is like religion to the goomba. He believes in his mother's marinara and Sunday sauce the same way he believes in the Virgin Mary—only more so. Insult his mother's cooking and you're a dead man. Some people just eat to live. The goomba, he lives to eat. You don't see the goomba taking a business meeting at Starbucks. He's going to suggest lunch at Luigi's or dinner at Mario's if he's serious.

I have a friend who everyone calls Big Rocco. He's a good friend and a great guy. And he's big. I mean, he's huge. He makes *me* look small. And he's always eating. And he's always excited about eating. You'd think a guy that big might be worried about his weight, or he might have eaten enough already that he wouldn't be too interested in the next meal. Not Big Rocco.

This guy is a perfect representative of the Goomba Diet. He eats everything, and he loves it.

A few years back Big Rocco went on the Atkins Diet. He was eating only meat. No macaroni. No bread. Just meat. But it was a special Big Rocco Atkins Diet. He'd go into a restaurant and make a big deal about how he was on this new food plan. He'd tell the waiter he couldn't eat any pasta. No carbohydrates! No sugar! No flour!

So he'd order the veal parmigiana. But then he'd say, "Double veal on that, all right?" Or he'd order the chicken marsala, and say, "Double chicken." He was like a guy going into a bar and saying, "Make mine a double!" Whatever he ordered, it had to be twice as much as the menu said.

It wasn't just in restaurants. He ate that way when he was in people's houses, too. He and his girlfriend went out to the Hamptons one summer to visit another friend of mine. He was still on the Atkins Diet, so he brought this suitcase filled with meat—steaks, sausages, ribs, hamburger, you name it. He took enough for thirty people.

The first day the three of them ate this huge meal for lunch—a giant Italian lunch, with seafood and roast chicken and steak and everything. Big Rocco got up from the table and said he was going to take a nap. He fell asleep on the sofa.

As soon as he was asleep, his girlfriend said to my friend, "Maybe you should start heating up the charcoal. He's going to be hungry later."

My friend was shocked. "Are you kidding? We just ate enough for ten people!"

"He's on the Atkins Diet," the girlfriend said. "He's going to be cranky if he wakes up and there's nothing to eat."

So my friend started the barbecue. Sure enough, Big Rocco woke up and sniffed the air and said, "Hey! Let's put something on the grill."

It was the same when he wasn't on the Atkins Diet. He'd go into a bar and, before he ordered a drink, he'd say, "You got any finger food?" He hasn't even got a cocktail yet and he's already ordering the Buffalo chicken wings.

In a restaurant, he'd order before the menu arrived. He'd say, "How about a pizza appetizer?" before the waiter even got there. Then he'd order a huge meal—rigatoni, chicken parmigiana, baked clams—and then he'd ask what's for dessert. If two or three different things sounded good, he'd order them all. "We'll share," he'd say. Then he'd eat all three of them himself.

What I love about this guy is his appetite, and what I really love is that it's not just about food. This guy has a great appetite for everything. He loves girls. He loves sports. He's always got tickets to the Knicks and the Nets and the Rangers and the Yankees. Plus he's generous—really generous. He's always calling and inviting you to go to the game with him. He entertains, too. He rents these big houses for the summer and has all his friends come out. This guy is living a big life and loving it.

Last summer I had this party on a boat. I rented a big boat, so me and a bunch of my friends could spend the day sailing around the Hudson and the East River. I invited about thirty people. I told them, "I'm taking care of the boat. You bring the food." I didn't tell anybody what to bring. I just said, "Bring something to eat."

Big Rocco went nuts. He went to Eli's, this great deli uptown, and ordered salads. I don't mean the little Styrofoam tubs of salad. I mean *platters* of salad. There was egg salad and potato salad and pasta salad. And, being Rocco, of course he brought dessert, too. There were these huge platters of cookies and cherries and Italian pastries.

Not only that, but when Rocco found out I had paid for the boat, he sent me a thank-you gift. A bottle of wine? No. It's Rocco. It was a *case* of wine.

Even a hungry guy like Rocco has certain foods he would never eat. Every goomba does. Some foods are just off-limits.

YOU'LL ALSO NEVER SEE A GOOMBA EAT . . .
- Any type of kabob
- Kraft American cheese singles
- Parfait
- SpaghettiOs
- Anything with the name "Franco-American" on it
- Hummus dip
- Home Pride Buttertop Bread
- Mayonnaise on French fries
- Lasagna out of a box

Excitement about eating isn't only a goomba thing. Even Shakespeare wrote about it. He said, "If music be the food of love, play on." But Old Shakey was wrong. *Food* is the food of love. Keep eating.

I don't think this comes from growing up without enough money. Big Rocco, for example, grew up in a pretty rich family. Me, I thought about food all the time when I was a kid. All my friends, too. We were always eating, or thinking about eating, or talking about eating. Sometimes, in a restaurant, we'd be eating lunch and talking about where we were going to eat dinner. This made the lunch taste better, and made us more excited about the dinner, too.

We were always scheming. We had tricks to get free food, to get more food, to steal candy, you name it. We talked about food a lot, too. Do non-goombas do that? I remember being a teenager and listening to guys talk about this restaurant or that restaurant. I don't think non-goomba kids do that. I have friends now, like from WASP families or Jewish families, and their kids don't seem to care about food one way or another.

When I was a kid I knew a guy named Billy. I'd bump into him on the street and he'd say, "Come on. Let's bounce around. Let's hit a few spots."

You've seen *The Godfather* and *Goodfellas*. You're probably imagining Billy was thinking of the Copa, or some of the night clubs, or some of the hot bars.

Not Billy. He'd say, "Let's start at the Pizza Palace." This was the pizza joint in my neighborhood. He'd go there and have a few slices.

Then he'd stop up the street at the hot dog stand. He'd take it easy there. He'd just have, like, one dog. Or two. With mustard and onions.

Then he'd hit the deli. He'd get a little provolone and maybe a piece of Italian bread. Maybe he'd get a sandwich, cheese and salami on the good Italian bread. (No mayo on that, by the way. The goomba doesn't mess up his salami with mayo. Mustard, yes; mayo, never.) Sometimes he might have the turkey, if it was fresh.

He'd throw some sun-dried tomatoes on there, and some lettuce, and sprinkle a little olive oil and some vinegar, and maybe add a hot Italian pepper—that's a sandwich.

He'd eat that standing up at the counter, looking at the soppressata and the prosciutto, talking to the people who work there.

Then he'd stop in at the drugstore, see who was hanging around. He might not eat anything there—just stop in and say hello. Then he'd step out again and maybe hit one of the luncheonettes or grocery stores.

In those days, Bath Avenue, the main street in the neighborhood where I grew up, was all Italian. Not like today. These days you drive along and you see Russian and Chinese—the grocery stores especially are all Chinese. In those days, no way. You wanted Chinese, you went to Chinatown. So the markets were all run by Italians and they all sold Italian products.

There was great food everywhere when we were growing up. We'd stop in at Emilio Brothers. We'd get a meatball sandwich. We'd get a sausage-and-peppers sandwich. Maybe we'd go to Chick's, which was another place in the neighborhood. They were famous for homemade pies. Incredible! We'd stop at Marino's Bakery for the bread. Or the pizza. Marino's had great pizza, too. Or, if we were really going to do it up and go to Ravioli Fair, we'd get them to make us a prosciutto-and-ricotta hero sandwich. That was heavy. That was living.

(Ravioli Fair is still a great place. A guy named Steve has run it for the last twenty-seven years. He sells the best cheeses and meats in the neighborhood. Fresh breads. Great sandwiches—meatball sandwiches, chicken parm, veal parm, he's got it all in there. The place is as good now as it was when I was a kid.)

So Billy would make the tour. He'd hit the spots. He'd spend $40 and eat like royalty.

I was playing a lot of ball in those days. I was skinny. I could eat like this and two days later be back down to my normal weight. I could eat like that twice a week and never notice it.

The Ravioli Fair gang.

These days, I have to watch it. I can't eat like that all the time.

Even if you are fat and need a diet, this one isn't necessarily right for you. You might not qualify as a goomba. For example:

THE GOOMBA DIET AIN'T FOR YOU IF . . .

- You've ever said, "Who wants *kugel*?"
- You've ever said, "I'll have the ham and pineapple pizza."
- You've ever said, "Chef Boyardee? All right!"
- You've ever even *thought* of saying, "Dang! We're out of Velveeta!"

Even on the days when I wasn't knocking around with guys like Billy, I could eat that kind of food, in that kind of variety, even in that quantity, without even leaving the house. On a Sunday, if there was going to be a big meal in the evening, maybe if there was family coming over, there wouldn't be any real lunch to speak of. We wouldn't sit down to a midday meal. Instead, there would be various foods laid out in a buffet. You'd cruise the buffet table and make a little plate for yourself.

There would be peppers stuffed with provolone. Or olives

stuffed with garlic. There would be rice balls or prosciutto balls. Potato croquettes. Meatballs. Fresh mozzarella. Soppressata. Italian olives. Fresh bread. You'd whack some of that together and make a plate. Lunch!

You want to take it easy. Remember, you got company coming. You don't want to overdo it. Your mother is going to be serving a big meal in a couple of hours. You've seen her in the kitchen all morning. You can smell what she's making in there. There's a roast beef or a roast chicken. There's sausages and peppers. There's the rest of the meatballs. She's got a tub of ricotta and she's stuffing shells. This is going to be a heavy meal.

Sunday mornings there was also bakery stuff. My mother would send me to the bakery for "buns." That meant whatever I liked or whatever looked best. I'd get jelly doughnuts, or crullers, or Italian pastries. I'd get a box of cookies.

Sometimes, my mother would send me for bagels and lox. We'd eat that on a Sunday morning, too. I grew up loving that stuff.

In other words, whatever's going on, the goomba is going to be eating. You will never, never hear a goomba say, "How can you eat at a time like this?" If it's a happy occasion, like a wedding or a birthday party, you're going to celebrate with food. If it's a sad occasion, like a funeral, you're going to compensate with food. If you're starting a relationship, if it's a first date or a first business meeting, you want to start it over a meal. If the relationship goes well, you celebrate your anniversary or the end of a successful transaction with a meal.

And if things don't go so well, well, there's food involved with that, too. If he's got a messy business situation, the goomba is going to start solving it over lunch. If he's got a messy romantic situation, he's going to try fixing it over dinner. If he wants to borrow money, or someone wants to borrow money from him, there's going to be a meal first. No matter what happens, it always happens around food.

This makes sense. If you're going to go into business with someone, or borrow money from someone, or go to bed with someone, you want to be friends with them first, right? So you break bread, have a talk, share some wine. That's going to make whatever comes later easier.

And everyone does this. The wise guys are eating in the expensive restaurants. The kids are going down to the deli. The grandmas are meeting for coffee and cake. The old guys are having espresso together after the bocce ball game. They're all lined up at Ravioli Fair, and Spumoni Gardens, and Nathan's. The only time a goomba isn't interested in food is at his *own* funeral.

GOOMBA DIET BASICS

For the average goomba, the average food plan is like this:

BREAKFAST: This isn't an important goomba meal. You get some coffee, maybe some eggs and a little bacon, you're done. Maybe a slice of toast. Maybe a muffin or something. It's not important. If you're the average goomba, you were out late last night banging around. You slept late. You got business to take care of. Lunch isn't far away. Forget breakfast.

LUNCH: Okay, now you're talking. Either this is a regular lunch or a special lunch. If it's a regular lunch, maybe you're eating with a friend, or with your family. You're not gonna spend the whole afternoon on this one. You got things to do. So you're going to eat light. You're going to start with a glass of red wine and a plate of macaroni—maybe a linguine with clams, maybe a penne à la vodka, maybe a simple spaghetti marinara. Then you're going to have some meat or chicken—a roast chicken, say, or some veal, or some steak, or some pork. Not too much, now. You'll probably have some vegetables with that—broccoli rabe, roast potatoes, something light like that. For dessert, an espresso and maybe a cannoli. That's it! A quick in and out.

If it's a special lunch, like an important business lunch, or a lunch with friends you haven't seen in a long time, or maybe you've got relatives in from out of town . . . that's different. Now you're going to have a *meal*.

The special lunch is going to look a lot like a regular lunch. There's just more of it. After the spaghetti marinara, or in addition to the spaghetti marinara, maybe there's a baked ziti. Before the steak or the chicken or the veal, maybe there's a plate of fried calamari, or a tray of baked clams. In addition to the steak or the chicken or the veal, there's more steak or chicken or veal. I was at a lunch with some friends recently and the waiter brought out a huge rack of veal chops. Unbelievable! We'd already eaten two kinds of pasta, two kinds of baked clams—one oreganata, one marinara—a minestrone soup and a *pasta e fagiole* soup. Then, with the veal chop, came broccoli rabe and a tray of roast potatoes with peppers and onions. I thought I was gonna die—or I had already died and gone to heaven! Then, just as we were finishing up the veal chops, the waiter came back with *another* plate of veal. This was veal chunks in a tomato cream sauce. Naturally, since we'd already finished all the roast potatoes, he brought another tray of those, too.

DINNER: Forget the special lunch. This is the big meal. This is the big event. This is what you eat on Sunday. This is what you eat on Friday night, if company is coming. This is what you eat in the restaurant when you've got people you really want to impress, or just people you really love to eat with.

It's a lot like the special lunch. But it's bigger. Imagine everything you get with the special lunch, but now there's more extra stuff. There's homemade meatballs in that spaghetti. There's two kinds of baked lasagna—regular and spinach. There's an eggplant marinara thrown in there somewhere. There's an eggplant parmigiana too, or a chicken parmigiana. Or, let's face it, both.

There's going to be a steak in there, too, or something special with beef, like a braciole. There's also going to be more seafood in there, like a dish with shrimp, or a dish with lobster—or both. There's going to be a chicken and a veal and a pork *and* steak. There's going to be three or four other vegetable things in there, too, to keep the broccoli rabe company.

Plus bread. No matter which meal you're eating, it goes best with a nice loaf of fresh Italian bread. This is so the goomba has something to do with his left hand other than talk. Your average American goomba, if he's got a healthy appetite, will always have a fork in one hand and a chunk of bread in the other. This is goomba etiquette. Unless you're cutting your steak, in which case you can put down the bread and pick up the knife.

And when dinner's done, there's going to be more dessert—cake, ice cream, and pastries in addition to the cannoli. There will be espresso, of course. But there will also be Sambuca or grappa.

A lot of people make fun of the goomba because he's a big guy. Maybe he's even a fat guy. Well, you try eating like that every day. You might put on a few pounds yourself. All those skinny guys with their South Beach and their Atkins and their protein drinks and their egg white omelettes—hey, try eating like a man for a couple of days and see what happens. You'll wind up with an appetite. You'll never eat another turkey burger in your whole life.

The goomba is also very selective about where he'll eat. He knows that no one's sauce is as good as his mother's. Even his wife doesn't make it quite right. This is just the rule. His best friend's mother doesn't either. No hard feelings. It's just the truth. His friend feels the same way about *his* mother's sauce, too. So when the goomba goes to his friend's house for dinner, he's not expecting too much. He loves the friend. He loves the friend's family. He just doesn't expect the food to be that good.

With restaurants, he's going to be careful, too. He won't eat anyplace that's not in the neighborhood, or hasn't been recommended to him by a goomba friend, or where he doesn't know the owners. Who eats with strangers? It might not be clean. Or, worse, it might not taste good. The goomba's paying for this meal. It's gotta be good.

So he's not going to go into any joint that pretends to be Italian when it's not, or pretends to serve "Italian" food when it doesn't. He is not eating at the Olive Garden. He is not eating at Buca di Beppo. He will absolutely not eat in a place that has the words "Authentic Italian" on the window or on the menu. If the outside of the restaurant says "Italian Cuisine," or "Fine Italian Cuisine," he ain't going in. He doesn't want cuisine. He wants some *food*. He'd rather eat Chinese than some phony Italian food in some phony joint called Luigi's Authentic Italian Kitchen, made by some *Amerigan*.

I drove by a place the other day that was called Pizza and Pastaria. Pastaria? What the hell is that? I couldn't even figure out how to pronounce it. So I wasn't going to eat there, obviously.

The average goomba isn't going to eat in any chain restaurants, either. He's especially not going to eat in any chain restaurants that pretend to be local neighborhood joints. So, you can just forget about anything like Denny's or Bob's Big Boy. He's not ordering pizza from Domino's, even if Domino's is the last pizza joint on Earth. And he's not going in for the chain specialty food, either, like fast-food falafel, ramen, or biscuits. Even if he knew what Australian food was, and he was interested in trying it, he ain't going into an Outback Steakhouse.

And even if he loves his kids, he'd probably die before he'd go into Chuck E. Cheese.

You probably won't catch him in any place with a clever name, either. The goomba's smart. He's not going into the Kopper Kitchen or the Cracker Barrel. He might be hungry, but he's not ever going to be *that* hungry.

Obviously food is the most important thing in the goomba's life after the love of his family. Some goombas, you get a look at how big they are, you might think food is even more important—they're huge, and they got small families. But even the hugest of the huge have their standards. They didn't get fat eating food they didn't like, right? Here are some more things the goomba will always avoid.

YOU WILL NEVER SEE A GOOMBA EAT . . .

- Possum.
- Pita.
- Pâté.
- Corn pone.

It's not just the food. The goomba has the same standards when it comes to beverages. He's gonna drink coffee. He's gonna drink sodas. He's especially going to drink a Manhattan Special—which is coffee and soda together, a sweet, carbonated espresso drink that comes from Brooklyn. They make it in Greenpoint. You used to be able to get it *only* in Brooklyn, Bensonhurst, Greenpoint, Staten Island, and down in Little Italy. This was long before Starbucks and the whole coffee craze. Nowadays you see the Manhattan Special in other places, and people who aren't even from Brooklyn drink it. For a while we had cases of it on the *Sopranos* set. You have a couple of those and bam! You don't need no Red Bull, pal. You're gone.

Of course the goomba is going to drink some wine, and maybe the occasional cocktail. There's stuff he won't drink, though, and I don't care how thirsty he is. For example . . .

YOU WILL NEVER SEE A GOOMBA DRINK . . .

- Ensure.
- Tang.
- A Zima.
- A Mimosa.

You could get a goomba completely drunk, so he doesn't even know his own name, but you will never hear him say, "Bartender! Another Pink Lady!" You will never hear a goomba say, "Can you make a Brandy Alexander?" He's not ever going to order a Tidy Bowl, or a Singapore Sling, or anything with crème de menthe in it. He is never going to ask anyone what's in a Sidecar, unless he's the bartender and some idiot just ordered one. You will never hear him explaining to anyone how to make a mint julep, or a hot toddy, unless that's his job. This would be like an elementary school goomba coming home and asking his goomba mother for a Tab, or a glass of Hawaiian Punch. It just isn't going to happen. The tab is what he runs at the bar. The Hawaiian Punch is what you're going to get from him if you're in Waikiki and you offer him a Pink Lady. No, wait a minute. He might be interested in that. You'd get the punch if you offered him a Fuzzy Navel or a Sloe Screw.

No matter what else is going on, food is the center of everything that happens in a goomba's life. And yet there are some times when eating is not appropriate.

GOOMBA DIET EATING ETIQUETTE
- It's OKAY to eat a hot dog at the ball game.
- It's NOT OKAY to eat a hot dog while you're actually playing in the game.
- It's OKAY to eat a big meal after having sex.
- It's NOT OKAY to eat while you're having sex.
- It's OKAY to ask, in a restaurant, "Are you going to finish that?"
- It's NOT OKAY to ask someone at another table.

Some goombas, of course, overdo it. They gotta go on a diet for real. This is a very sad thing for the goomba.

I decided a while back that I wanted to lose a little weight. I went on some kind of diet. It worked, too. I started eating less. I started exercising more. I started losing weight. Then one of the producers from *The Sopranos* took me aside. He said, "You're on a diet, huh? It looks good. Only, don't lose any more weight, all right?" He didn't want the fat character I play to get too skinny.

That was all I needed to hear. I started eating again. Not going nuts. Just eating normal.

That's not good enough for some guys. I have one friend whose weight was starting to be a medical problem. He couldn't stop this compulsive overeating. So he went in for one of those operations where they staple part of your stomach closed. Or whatever they do. I don't know the details, but the point is, then you can't overeat. You eat a slice of pizza, you're done. You eat a hamburger, you're done. Try to eat more and you get sick to your stomach. You can eat again in an hour, but you couldn't eat again right away without throwing up.

Well, guess what? My friend figured out some way to beat the system. He figured out some way to overcome being sick to his stomach and thinking he was going to throw up. He had his stomach stapled, he started losing weight, and then he started *gaining* weight.

What is it with a guy like that? Is he compensating for something? I've heard of people who do that—eat because they don't have enough love, or money, or attention, or whatever. I've even seen people do that. I remember hearing guys in Vegas say, "I got killed at the blackjack table, but I made up for it at the buffet. I ate, like, a hundred shrimp." If they ever stopped to calculate what those shrimp cost them, they'd blow their brains out. Getting that free buffet made them feel a little better about losing a thousand dollars trying to hit a 17.

Some guys will go to all kinds of extremes. I knew one guy who built a second kitchen in his house, in the upstairs hall, next to his bedroom. It had a refrigerator, a freezer, and a microwave. That way he didn't have to get up and go all the way to the kitchen downstairs when he woke up in the middle of the night and needed a snack. He could just walk out his bedroom door and grab something and eat it in bed. He'd eat a half-gallon of ice cream like that, or a quart of peanut butter, straight out of the jar. He'd order these tiny cheeseburgers—like those White Castle burgers—that you could heat in the microwave. He'd eat a dozen of them, just like that.

These are guys with an eating problem. Or several eating problems. They need the Goomba Diet! Here are some rules they could follow that would help them:

PROBLEM: You eat your deli sandwich so fast you get a stomachache.
SOLUTION: Take the paper off the sandwich before you eat it.

PROBLEM: Your doctor says you're too fat.
SOLUTION: Get a new doctor.

PROBLEM: You're so fat, your friends start calling you Big Angelo.
SOLUTION: Have a son. Call him Little Angelo.

Like I said, most goombas aren't into foreign food. They'll eat Chinese, but that's about it. Try to get a goomba into a Hungarian restaurant, or an Armenian restaurant, or even a Japanese restaurant. He'll say, "Let's get a slice." Ask him if he wants to go get some *paella*, or some *pistou*, and he'll say, "I don't eat Mexican food." He ain't eating no bratwurst, no bangers and mash, no baguette, and no *boeuf bourguignonne*. He's not going to eat any mutton. Forget anything with *filo* dough. Forget your *schwarma*, your falafel, your spanakopita. What is that, Arab? He ain't going near it.

And why should he? Food-wise, the goomba is born into the Garden of Eden. Why should he be tempted by the apple? Why should he ever eat anything other than what his mother and his grandmother feed him?

My friend Kip Addotta grew up in an Italian neighborhood, just like me. His Uncle Victor ran a poker game on Flatbush Avenue for more than forty years. He'd hold the game every two weeks, and it would last days. Victor would bring in food and booze, and set up cots. He'd play in the games and pull 5 percent of every pot. The games were legendary. Everyone came, from mayors to Mafia guys. When Kip was a kid, the Bonanno brothers bounced him on their knees.

Kip remembers that in those days very few households had telephones. If you wanted your friend to come out and play, you went into the street and yelled at his house, "Hey, Tommy!" Usually his mother would come to the door and tell you Tommy was coming down in a minute.

Then she'd always ask you to come inside and wait. She'd take you through the house into the kitchen. A big pot of sauce would always be simmering on the stove. The mother would always tear off a hunk of nice Italian bread and dip it in the sauce and give you that to eat while you waited.

There was nothing better, ever, than that bread with that sauce. And then you'd go out and play.

If you grew up like that, why would you ever eat anything else?

My only eating problem is I'm very particular. I like what I like and I insist on eating well. If I'm not in New York or Las Vegas or Atlantic City, this could be a problem. If I'm in, say, Atlanta, it's a *big* problem.

Il Cortile, in New York's Little Italy, is my favorite place in the world. I could eat dinner there seven nights of the week, plus squeeze in a few lunches. The owners are like family to me. I eat everything on the menu and I never get tired of it.

This devotion to restaurants runs in the family. My daughter Bria loves The Palm in Las Vegas. If we're going, she knows we're going to have a big meal. She's tall and skinny, and I don't know where she puts it. But if we're going to the Palm, she'll say, "We're gonna have a *feast* tonight." She'll order an appetizer and a steak and a side dish and then a dessert. And why not? She knows how to have a good time. She's social, and she likes going out, and she likes a loud place, just like I do.

It's not just me and my family. When I was sitting down to write this book, I called some of the actors on *The Sopranos*. I asked them to describe their idea of a perfect evening. Here's what they said:

"Drinking and eating for hours with friends, in a restaurant or in someone's house," said Michael Imperioli, who plays Tony Soprano's lieutenant Christopher Moltisanti on the show. "Nice company. Nice wine. A couple of courses of really good food. Lots of laughs. That's a great evening."

"Good friends, and great food," said Lorraine Bracco, who plays Tony's psychiatrist, Dr. Melfi, on the show. "Good conversation. Doesn't matter where."

"I like to sit around and eat and talk, with people," said Vincent Pastore, who played "Big Pussy" Bonpensiero in the early episodes of the show. "I like to go to dinner with a girl."

Do you start to notice a theme here? Ask a goomba his idea of a perfect evening. Young or old, male or female, you're going to hear the same thing. Food, friends, and a few laughs.

The same is true for me. Even now, with everything I have going on in my life, my favorite thing in the world is to get together with a couple of good friends and spend the evening in a restaurant. And I've always got company. Take my friend Vince Curatola. He and his wife like nothing better than a spur-of-the-moment dinner. He'll call from his car, driving in from Jersey, and say, "Stevie— you eat yet? I'll meet you in forty-five minutes."

Me and my wife will meet him and his wife at Il Cortile, maybe

Tell me, what's better than a big plate of calamar'?

with another guy from the show, and we'll make an evening of it. What do we do? Order another bottle of white wine. Order another plate of those shrimp. We eat and laugh and talk about how lucky we are to be living such good lives.

If that sounds good to you, keep reading. The next few chapters of *The Goomba Diet* will show you how to make my lifestyle *your* lifestyle.

CHAPTER 2

Goomba Moderation and Exercise

All of this eating in restaurants could make you fat. If this happens, don't panic. Don't go nuts. Don't stop eating. And don't stop reading. This is Phase Two of the Goomba Diet, the part where we talk about moderation and exercise.

"Moderation" is a big word for some goombas, I know. And a scary word. So is "exercise." Don't worry. This is *goomba* moderation and exercise. This is the only area of a goomba's life where he doesn't go overboard. We're not going to get carried away here. Moderation is the only thing the goomba does in moderation.

The average goomba looks like an unhealthy guy. His idea of putting more iron in his diet is carrying a gun in his belt. To him, "Low Fat" is just a guy he knows in Chinatown. "Non Fat" milk is what a non-fat guy might drink. The average goomba's exercise program is limited to cranking back the La-Z-Boy recliner and reaching for the remote. He might have a big workout on the day he loses the remote. The goomba's idea of heavy lifting is picking up a copy of *The Da Vinci Code*. If he wants to lose weight, he'll go to an Olive Garden for a couple of meals in a row—because a real goomba is practically allergic to that junk.

There's nothing wrong with living that way. Most goombas eat a balanced diet. They choose from the four food groups—ravioli, cannelloni, manicotti, and lasagna. They eat like everybody else in America. You take a piece of Italian bread, a slice of prosciutto, a slice of mozzarell' and what have you got? It's a goomba cheeseburger.

Eating that way, the average goomba gets a certain amount of exercise, even if he's lifting his fork a lot more often than he's lifting free weights. Is it enough? Maybe not. The goomba might need to break a sweat, too.

To get started, here are some exercises you can do at home or around the neighborhood:

GOOMBA DIET EXERCISES
- Touch your toes: If this is difficult, pay a guy to do it for you.
- Try running cross-country: Take a flight to Vegas.
- Twelve-ounce curls: Get a bottle of beer. Lift. Repeat. Switch hands. Repeat.
- Work out with a dumbbell: Any idiot will do.
- Work out with a gymnast: Or any girl who's good in bed.

Most of your adult goombas are not into sports. Not anymore. They watch the Yankees or the Mets or the Knicks or the Rangers, but you don't find these guys actually playing sports themselves. Lots of them did when they were kids—*all* the guys from my neighborhood did. We had softball leagues and basketball leagues.

There are exceptions, of course. If you go over to Dyker Park in Brooklyn, where I played basketball as a kid, you'll see twenty

Me with some of the bocce guys, at Dyker Park.

or thirty guys right now playing bocce ball. Most of them are over sixty. They take the game very seriously, too. They have to— they're playing for money. They play for anywhere from $2 a man to $10 a man, on two-man teams. You'll see them put dice into a metal cup and shake it around. When they pour it out, that decides who's on what team. Then the partners start throwing the bocce balls. Whoever gets to twelve points first is the winner. You could be up or down $200 by the end of the day.

They're serious about the game. You go out there in the winter, you'll see them shoveling the snow to clear the court. This is their whole life. When they get too old for bocce, no problem. There's some guys over there, even older, who play pinochle all day long. For money. Come rain or shine.

That's the goomba way—all the way in. When I was a teenager, sports was the most important thing in my life. I dreamed about baseball. I knew every statistic about every player on every team. I could tell you more about every single team in the National or

American league from the 1970s than I could about *any* team today, including the Yankees.

When I played baseball, I never missed a game, even when I knew I wasn't going to play. Even if it was raining, I'd go to the field to see if the game was rained out. In those days, someone from the team had to go to the park first thing in the morning to reserve the field, or else some other team would get it. I used to meet the coach and help save the field. We'd go over there at five in the morning and sit in his car waiting for the other guys to come.

I was obsessed with sports. It was all I thought about. There were times when all I thought about was basketball. I would rather play basketball than do anything else—and I mean anything.

Then things happened. I got older. Same thing with most of my friends. Most of them are too busy now to play any sports—or too fat, or too old, or too tired, or all of that.

These days, I'm still into sports—but only as a spectator. I don't actually play sports anymore.

In the old days, my wife and I used to go out and try our luck at the batting cage. That was kind of fun. One time we got tennis rackets and started hitting the ball at each other. On the court, I mean. That didn't last. I even tried bowling. I would bounce it down the alley like Fred Flintstone, but I couldn't hit the pins. So that didn't last either.

So for a while I got really into reading about sports. I read every baseball biography and autobiography I could find. When I was a kid, I knew more about Mickey Mantle than anybody alive except maybe Mickey Mantle. Now I learned about guys like Ty Cobb and Ted Williams. Giant men, unbelievable.

When I got tired of that, I read true crime. My wife said I was insane, because reading the books made me so mad. I'd read these stories and I'd want to go find the criminals and kill them with my bare hands.

So I stopped doing that.

I still read. My idea of a good time, when I'm on the road, is sometimes nothing more than ordering room service and sitting in my underwear and reading a book. And it's not what you'd think. I read everything by David Sedaris. Then I read some stuff by Augusten Burroughs. This is not the typical goomba reading material, I know.

I've read all the mob books, too, of course. I was interested in it. Not infatuated, the way some guys are, because I already know all that stuff. I grew up around it. I wasn't reading it like a how-to book, or a training manual on how to live my life. Some guys do. Some goombas think you should actually try to behave like Michael Corleone to get ahead in life. I think that's nuts. I am not a gangster. I am not a wise guy. Those people are criminals. They make their living by hurting and taking advantage of people weaker than them. Why would I want anyone to think I'm one of those people?

Most of my goomba friends are not big book readers. I've had people tell me, in all honesty, "The only book I ever read in my life was your book, Steve." And nothing in the world gives me a bigger thrill than knowing that someone who never read a book read *my* book, and liked it.

Also like most of my goomba friends, I don't have many hobbies. I don't think hobbies are a goomba deal.

There are exceptions. My friend Vince Curatola recently celebrated his birthday by buying himself a Harley-Davidson Road King Classic. He already has a couple of fancy cars and he dotes on them like they're museum pieces. Then he bought the Harley. So what did he do? He organized a fund-raising Harley ride, got nine hundred other bikers out for a Sunday cruise, and raised $115,000 for charity.

Some guys I know are collectors. My friend Joe Soup—Joe Gannascoli, also a member of the *Sopranos* cast—collects bobblehead dolls. I have no idea why, but he's very proud of his collection. He has bobble heads of all the mascots of all the professional sports teams—the Indian guy with the Atlanta Braves and the seal

My pals Joe, "The Bobble Head Collector," and Michael.

for the San Francisco Giants. He has hundreds of them.

He also collects baseball cards—but only for players named Joe. Seriously. He has Joe Pepitone and Joe Torre and all the other Joe's you can imagine. He recently bought a new house, and he's going to finish out the basement and make a museum down there for all his bobble heads and all his Joe cards.

Another guy I know collects Batman and Superman stuff. Dolls. Books. Comic books. Masks. Halloween costumes.

I'm happy for him. I just don't understand how a grown man gets involved with something like collecting miniature Supermans. But this guy has filled an entire room at his parents' house.

I can't see me doing that. I can't see me doing a lot of things. Here's a list of hobbies that are probably not good for the goomba, and are definitely not part of the Goomba Diet. Why not? Because they take valuable time away from the things that are really important—like food and family.

BAD GOOMBA HOBBIES
- Bird-watching. (Goombas watch TV and broads.)
- Hang gliding. (Goombas fly only in airplanes that have first-class sections, even if they're flying coach.)
- Mountain biking. (Picture your favorite goomba. Picture him on a bike. No way.)
- Anything called X-Treme. (Unless it would be X-Treme Cuisine.)
- Anything that involves yarn.

Me and NY Giants' Michael Strahan at the fourth season premiere.
He's an honorary goomba.

Sports and exercise are an important part of any diet, and the Goomba Diet is no exception. If the goomba is going to keep up a healthy appetite, and have a reason to maintain his beautiful collection of jogging suits, he's going to need to break a sweat now and then. But you gotta be careful here. Some sports come naturally to the goomba and some don't. Here are some helpful guidelines:

GOOD SPORTS FOR GOOMBAS
- Baseball.
- Football.
- Basketball.
- Bocce ball.
- Pool.
- The numbers.

BAD SPORTS FOR GOOMBAS
- Luge.
- Lacrosse.
- Fencing.
- Frisbee.
- Water polo.

I'm not saying there's anything wrong with that stuff. I'm not even saying the goomba wouldn't be good at it. He could be good at anything he puts his mind to. It's just that no self-respecting goomba is going to sign up for those sports unless maybe there was money in it or it was a way to get laid. I had a friend who took up sky-diving, for example, because he was in love with this girl who was into it, and the girl told him she could never be interested in a guy who didn't dive. Then she dropped him anyway. Not out of the plane. She just stopped seeing him. So now he feels like an idiot.

The bottom line on exercise should be doing what you like doing. Anything that gets the cardiovascular system going, and doesn't hurt somebody else, that's good exercise.

Unless, of course, it's embarrassing. There are certain types of exercise that you will never see a goomba do:

BAD EXERCISES FOR GOOMBAS
- Croquet.
- Crochet.
- Synchronized swimming.
- Anything involving chaps.

Even the more mainstream sports are not necessarily right for the athletic goomba. Like, I don't know any goombas who play golf. The goomba isn't investing eight hours to take a walk and hit a little white ball around. He isn't playing tennis, either. He isn't at the club. He isn't going horseback riding or playing polo. That's all WASP stuff, and maybe good for Jewish guys who are too young for pinochle. But you won't find the goomba around Bushwood Country Club, unless they have a poker room. You might find him at the pool, but he's tanning and smoking a Cohiba and drinking a *mojito*. He doesn't own jodhpurs. He isn't at the rodeo or throwing horseshoes. He doesn't own a saddle. That's all hillbilly stuff and cowboy stuff. I can guarantee you will never see a goomba playing a banjo.

One good way to tell whether the activity is good for goombas or not: If there's a picture of it in an L.L. Bean catalog, the goomba ain't doing it. He's not camping or going in a kayak or a canoe. He's not wearing snowshoes, or deck shoes, or cross-country skis. He's not rock climbing, or mountain climbing, or doing anything that involves ropes and knots—unless, maybe, he's into that stuff in the bedroom.

The goomba isn't doing anything they show on the X Games. There's no snowboarding in the goomba world. There's no motocross. All those sports you see at the "World's Strongest Man" competitions—forget it. The goomba is not going to carry a wagon, or try to lift a 300-pound chunk of marble over his head. If he needs to do something like that, he hires some guys.

And any sport that involves travel, that ain't happening, either. The only time you'll find the goomba in the Arctic Circle is if that's the name of an ice cream parlor. You might find him in the Amazon, but only if that's a strip club that features big broads.

Anything you see President Bush doing, he's not doing that. He ain't jogging or riding a mountain bike. Same with George Bush Senior. He isn't going to Kennebunkport. He isn't going sailing.

It's nothing personal. He's just not into those things. He's not playing volleyball, or badminton, or squash. He might be a bowler, but he's more likely to be throwing dice than strikes and spares. His idea of strenuous exercise might be filling an inside straight or holding out for a flush on the river. His idea of a big workout might be hitting the numbers or putting a grand on the four the hard way in Vegas.

A great goomba sport? Texas Hold-Em.

But a man's got to stay in shape, right? Here are some more Goomba Diet exercise ideas:

- Can't get motivated to run? Don't pay your bookie.
- Go to Vegas. Build up your biceps by playing only the nickel slots.
- Work those abs. Raise and lower the La-Z-Boy while watching the Jets.
- Bench press all your sister's wedding albums at once.
- Have more sex with the *goomar*. Have sex with your wife, too.
- *Walk* to court.

If you don't work out, and you let yourself go, pretty soon you won't be good for anything. If you eat too much, you won't be able to eat anymore. If you get too fat, you won't be able to leave the house. You read those stories in the paper every once in a while about some guy who gets so fat that he can't get out his own front door. The paramedics or the fire department have to remove a wall in order to get him to the hospital. Can you imagine? I knew a guy once who was so fat that his wife had to drive him to the mall every time he wanted to take a crap: He was too big to sit on his own toilet. So his wife had to drive him ten miles to a shopping center where they had one of those special, handicapped toilets.

Here's a worse story. I grew up with a guy who had to be taken to the zoo to be weighed. When he got sick and needed an MRI, they took him to the Bronx Zoo to use the MRI machine they use for the elephants.

That's when you know it's time to put down the cannoli.

To me, that would be like going to hell. I mean, I'd die if I couldn't eat. So I try to watch it.

It's still possible that the goomba might get carried away and wind up weighing too much. He can't fit into his own clothes anymore. He's gotta do something. If it's an emergency like this, he might have to change his diet.

Now, the average goomba lives on a pretty strict diet already. There are certain foods he will never eat, no matter what. The following foods are not on the Goomba Diet.

BAD FOODS FOR GOOMBAS
- Oscar Mayer Lunchables
- McDonald's Filet-O-Fish
- Franco-American SpaghettiOs
- Cheez Whiz
- Egg Beaters
- TV dinners

If you are eating any of those foods, don't. Stop the insanity! Put down the fork!

If the goomba keeps getting fatter, maybe he's gotta slow down a little. Maybe he needs to take it easy on the groceries. But how? Most goombas aren't clear on the dieting concept. You tell them they should eat more whole foods and they'll start eating foods with holes in 'em—bagels and doughnuts and onion rings.

But even the goomba can make some changes in his eating habits without violating the principles of the Goomba Diet. Here are some tips—nothing drastic, like Pritikin or Atkins or South Beach. Just some suggestions:

GOOMBA DIET WEIGHT-LOSS TIPS
- At lunch, have the baked clams *or* the fried calamar'—not both.
- Stop eating all that pasta. From now on, only ravioli and manicotti.
- Eat more vegetables. Every time you have a slice, ask for extra tomato sauce.
- Eliminate red meat. Cook it until it's brown.
- Avoid fast food. Slow it down by parking and going inside to order.
- Remember the scene in *The Godfather* where, right after Paulie's assassination, Clemenza says, "Leave the gun. Take the cannoli."? Practice saying, "Leave the gun. *Leave* the cannoli."

If a couple of weeks of that doesn't take the extra pounds off, you might have to get drastic. You might have to start exercising.

Don't be alarmed. It's not that bad. It's all a question of balance. Don't overdo it! Remember, if you exercise too much, you're only going to get hungry again. So don't go crazy. Here are some more exercises you can do:

MORE GOOMBA DIET EXERCISE TIPS
- Get a stationary bike: Find a bike that's stationary. Steal it. Ride it around.
- Practice muscle control: Call the guy who does your rough stuff and order him around a little.

- Pick up something heavy: Ask a fat broad for her phone number.
- Avoid sugar: Don't call your *goomar* for a week.

Maybe weight loss isn't for you, anyway. Not everybody is supposed to be skinny. Look at me. If I was littler, I might not have been cast as Bobby Bacala in the first place.

This fat guy's doing all right for himself.

CHAPTER 3

Eat Right to Live Right

I loved the idea of going out for dinner ever since I was a little kid. My parents had been crazy about restaurants and nightclubs, and spent a lot of time in places like the Copa—before they had children. I couldn't wait to grow up and start living like that.

By the time I was a teenager, I was beginning to go out and have fun on my own. Even when I had almost no money, I was spending what I had on having a good time. Me and my friends would go to these seafood restaurants in Sheepshead Bay, and we would eat like kings. It might be all the money we had in the world, but we were going to enjoy it. We were seventeen-year-old guys acting like big shots. We'd order the clams and the fried calamari. You'd get your choice of mild, medium, or hot sauce for the calamar', and you'd eat until you were stuffed.

Food was always part of the fun. When I was older, when I was going out to the clubs, the evening always started and ended with

A young skinny goomba on the ball field—that's me, third from the right.

food. In the middle you'd be drinking or dancing or chasing some girl, but the beginning and the ending was always food.

Before we went out, we'd usually meet someplace for a slice or a sandwich. We'd meet at the Ravioli Fair for a prosciutto and mozzarella. Or we'd meet at Spumoni Gardens for pizza. You'd get some food in you so you weren't drinking on an empty stomach.

Some guys take their pizza very seriously. They are passionate about pizza, and they'll argue until they're blue in the face about which pizza is the best in the city, which means the best in the world. Totonno's in Coney Island is a favorite. Patsy's in Manhattan is big. Lombardi's, on Spring Street in Little Italy, people will tell you it was the first pizza place in the country, so it's the best. To me, it's L & B Spumoni Gardens, hands down.

Maybe it's genetic. My father went to Spumoni Gardens when he was a kid. I went to Spumoni Gardens when I was a kid. I remember sitting on those benches when I was in elementary school, having that great pizza. When I was eleven or twelve, I played baseball for the Ty Cobbs. This was a big deal. If you were good enough to be on the Ty Cobbs, you were somebody. If you had that Ty Cobb jacket, people knew you were somebody. On the weekends, we'd play two or three games. Afterward, we'd go over to Spumoni Gardens. They had a lot of good things on the menu, but I was always a pizza guy. I never ate anything else. Always the square pizza—the round is okay, I guess, but I only eat the square—and then the pistachio spumoni for dessert.

When I was older, I liked nothing better than starting the evening with a square of pizza and then going out on the town.

Then, after a night in the clubs, you'd either go to a diner and eat their greasy hamburgers or you'd go to Coney Island, to Nathan's, and get two or three hot dogs. (We always went to the one in Coney Island, by the way. Never the other Nathan's.) After a night out, there was nothing tastier than some good junk food like that.

These days, you're probably not going to find me eating at Nathan's at three o'clock in the morning, but you'll still find me at Spumoni Gardens for dinner. I still go there all the time. Even when I lived in Las Vegas, we'd visit New York and I would actually make the driver go through that part of Brooklyn on the way into Manhattan—which is not exactly taking a short cut into the city. I had a slice there recently with a friend who'd never eaten real Brooklyn pizza before. We were sitting outside. The sun was shining. The restaurant was crowded. We ate our pizza. He said, "That's great pizza. One slice, and I'm totally satisfied."

I said, "Me, too." Then I went and got another piece.

That's the problem. Like I said before, you can get carried away with the food thing. If you have two pieces of pizza every time you have one, you're going to wind up with a weight problem. Then you won't be able to have any pizza at all.

So let this be a cautionary tale.

I've got a friend who is such an overeater that he eats with both hands. I don't mean like a piece of bread in his left hand and a fork in his right hand. I mean an Italian sandwich in his left hand and a piece of pizza in his right hand. This is a guy who works up a sweat eating. It's like aerobics with him—grab the macaroni, get a piece of chicken, eat the chicken, grab a steak, cut the steak, grab some calamar'—while talking and drinking wine and mopping it all up with bread at the same time. I like my dinner just like the next man, but this guy puts me off my food. I said to him one time, "Slow down. You're making me sick." He said, "I'm sorry. I had a light lunch."

That's another guy who needs the Goomba Diet.

It's easy for the average person to know when he's eating too much. For the goomba, who has a bigger appetite, it might be a little harder. Here are some warning signs:

YOU MIGHT BE OVEREATING IF . . .

- You take your kids to the zoo and they start throwing peanuts . . . at you.
- You order food with your mouth full.
- You eat sausages *and* meatballs. For breakfast.
- You had to buy a bigger belt more than once this year.

Part of the problem with the Goomba Diet is that most goombas are Italian and most Italians eat only Italian food. Now, there might be a lot of good Italian food you can eat that's not fattening. But I've never seen any of it. Most of what I like to eat, in the quantities that I like to eat it, will make you heavy. I know you're not supposed to eat too many carbohydrates. But try telling that to a plate of fettuccine Alfredo or spaghetti carbonara. I know you're not supposed to eat too much bread. But if we weren't meant to eat bread, why is there prosciutto and mozzarella? I mean, what else is bread *for*?

I've tried eating less. But I enjoy life more when I'm eating better—when I'm eating more of what I want, not more of what I think is good for me.

Maybe I look better, too. People in the entertainment business will tell you that you need to be thin if you're going to be on television. "TV puts on ten pounds," they say, because the camera supposedly makes you look fatter than you are.

Jim Gandolfini strikes a pose.

If you're already a big guy, like me, TV is supposed to make you look really huge. And most people would say that really huge is not attractive. Who wants to go around with a fat guy?

Well, here's the funny thing. Being on TV may make you look a little heavier. But being on TV makes you look *a lot* sexier, too.

I joke about that sometimes with Jim Gandolfini, the star of *The Sopranos*. Like me, he's a big guy. And we like to say, "TV doesn't put ten pounds on you. It takes fifty pounds *off* you." Being on TV makes you attractive.

I'm a married guy. I don't fool around. So I really don't care one way or the other. But I know what has happened to me since I've been on the show. The bottom line is, I've never been propositioned so much in my life.

It happens in restaurants, on the street, in clubs, in casinos, at parties, and at premieres. Wherever I go, people pay more attention than they did before I was on TV. Some of them are women, and some of the women are paying me that special kind of attention.

Sometimes it's ridiculous. I was in a club one night and girls were coming up to me, giving me their phone numbers, acting very bold. Then the deejay said, "Come on down, girls! We got a guy here from *The Sopranos.* Come on and show Steve Schirripa your stuff!"

This was a charity event—a fund-raiser for a very worthy cause. It wasn't like a strip club or anything. But all the girls started pulling up their tops. I had ten or fifteen girls come over and ask me to sign their tits.

I don't go for that kind of stuff, and I didn't sign anybody's anything, but I guess I understand it. In our culture, we treat famous people like they're special. We treat all famous people like they're beautiful. So, for some girl working in an office, making $22,000 a year and living in some crappy apartment, maybe getting friendly with some guy from a TV show would be a pretty big deal. She'd get to tell her friends about it. Maybe my life seems glamorous to a girl like that.

I guess that's one of the perks of the job to some people. That's part of the allure of being an actor, or a rock star, or a politician, or just rich. I'm not saying this is what Donald Trump does, but it must have occurred to him at some point in his life that he was getting more action after he was rich than he did before he got rich.

I'm not saying I never got any action before *The Sopranos,* but I definitely didn't have girls lining up asking me to autograph their bodies.

Not for nothing, but it's not just me. Stevie Van Zandt, who plays Silvio on the show, gets the same kind of attention. He was a skinny guy his whole life, when he toured as a rock and roll musician. For *The Sopranos,* to play Silvio, he gained about sixty pounds—on purpose. He said it really changed the way he walks and talks and acts, and that it helped him play that part. He said it was really fun to be that heavy, for a while—even if he can't get rid of the weight now.

We were talking about TV putting on the extra weight, and I asked him, "What about the broads?" He said, "I've been a rock star my whole life. The women have always been plentiful. The difference now is the *hair* is higher."

Back when I was single I woulda been pretty happy about this. Now? What are you gonna do? It's just kind of embarrassing.

And I'm not even the star of the show. When Gandolfini goes out, it's ridiculous. Women *throw* themselves at him.

One night, near the end of the first year of the show, Terry Winter, one of the writers on the show, was out with Gandolfini. Terry's Scottish, but he grew up surrounded by Italians, so he's really more Italian than anything else (he once told me that if there was a war between Scotland and Italy, he'd be on the side serving macaroni). Terry said, "How does it feel to know every woman in this place wants to fuck you?" Gandolfini said, "They don't want to fuck me. They want to fuck Tony Soprano. Where were they ten years ago, when I couldn't get laid to save my life?"

Vinnie Pastore, who used to play Big Pussy on the show, says the same thing. "I used to walk in my neighborhood and no girl would even look at me. Now, the same girls act like they want to sleep with me. For what? Because I'm a star now? What if I was a garbageman? It's not even exciting to me anymore. Now, I'm like, *Where were you when I needed you?*"

He's probably right. Would he be getting that much attention if he was, like, a plumber? I don't think so. Would I be getting all this attention if I was still a bouncer? I don't think so.

But that's what celebrity does. It makes you beautiful. Like Terry Winter says, "The guys on the show are like rock stars—in certain parts of New York and New Jersey. They're like the Beatles of New Jersey."

So sometimes, when I get the idea that I should be worried about how I look, I stop worrying. I see how people react. Girls are very intrigued. I'm no sex symbol, but like I said before, there's a lot of skinny actors out of work, going to auditions, tending bar at night, wearing black turtlenecks and quoting Chekhov—and not getting laid.

In the end, does it matter why someone finds you attractive?

Most guys probably wouldn't care—as long as the girls are interested. Is it me, or is it the part I play on TV? Most guys would think, "Hey, I'll be Gilligan if that's what you want."

Still, you don't want to push your luck. Marlon Brando was the sexiest man alive long before *People* magazine had a "Sexiest Man Alive." Look what happened to him! Like the Goodyear blimp. Elizabeth Taylor was the most beautiful woman ever to make a movie. Look what happened to her! Like the Fuji blimp.

So I try to keep an eye on my food. I try to stay on the Goomba Diet.

Your average goomba, his idea of dieting is waiting until after dinner to have dessert. His idea of working off a big meal is snoring in front of the TV with his mouth open and his hand in his pants.

Here are a few more ideas for keeping the extra pounds off:

MORE GOOMBA DIET TIPS

- Try an appetite suppressant. Eat in an Armenian restaurant.
- Try more exercise. Walk to the refrigerator yourself instead of yelling, "Honey! Get me another beer!"
- Change your routine. Try substituting alfalfa sprouts for macaroni. *I'm kidding!*
- Change your habits. Try actually sweating in your sweat suit.
- Cut out between-meal snacking. If you need a slice between breakfast and lunch, make sure to refer to it as "brunch."

When I was a kid my mother was very strict at the table. She had strong ideas about table manners. Many's the time I got smacked

P. Diddy and my mom. Don't ask. I have no idea.

or yelled at for saying the wrong thing or doing the wrong thing during dinner.

Her weapon of choice was the wooden spoon. If you were whining at the table, or picking on your younger brother, which I did all the time, whack! A smack in the head.

I knew kids who got "punished," where the mother would call the father and tell him you'd done something bad, and she'd say, "Wait until your father gets home," and then the dad would take off his belt and say, "This is going to hurt me more than it's going to hurt you. . . ."

No. Not in my house. In my house, you got it right here, right now. Smack in the head with the wooden spoon.

We helped out in the kitchen. We had to help set the table, help clean off the table. Everybody had a job. My job was to take out the garbage.

This was a bad job, because the garbage can was so far away. You had to take the garbage bag downstairs, out the front door, and around the corner. And then there was no place to put it. The cans would be full. There was never any room for it.

This was very challenging, for an idiot kid like me. So I found a solution. There was this guy on the block that I didn't like. I'd walk over to his house and throw the bag of garbage into his front yard.

One time he went through the bag and found an envelope with our address on it. Of course he came to our house and wanted to know who was throwing our trash in his front yard. And I caught hell for that. What a genius I was!

The lessons I didn't get from my mother I got from my coaches. They were always trying to teach us how to behave.

My college basketball coach would sometimes take us out to dinner after the ball games. We'd sit in a restaurant. He would teach us how to act. He'd say, "Don't be a slob. Put your napkin in your lap. Get your elbows off the table. Don't be rude. Talk when it's your turn. Leave a tip for the waiter." He was teaching us how to be human beings.

A lot of goombas didn't grow up with my mother, or my coaches, so they didn't grow up with good manners. Most goombas I know eat like animals. They belch so loud it sets off the car alarms in the neighborhood. They think that making dinner table conversation means arranging two meatballs and a sausage on their plate and saying, "Hey, what does this look like?"

Well, it's never too late. Any goomba can learn how to eat like a gentleman, or at least how to stop eating like a pig. Here are some guidelines for proper table etiquette:

GOOMBA DIET TABLE MANNERS
- If someone asks you to say grace, don't make a crucifix out of a pair of breadsticks.
- While you're saying grace and the other people have their eyes closed, don't steal an extra sausage.
- Don't put two meatballs in your cheeks and do your Don Corleone impression.

- Don't floss right after the meal with the string tied around the roast chicken.
- No matter what kind of argument breaks out, remember: Food is not a weapon. Put down that leg of lamb.

I've been to a lot of goomba households where the kids are unruly. Why do people raise their children like that? The kids are shouting at the table and disrespecting their parents and their grandparents. Doesn't anyone tell the kids this is wrong? Doesn't anyone tell their parents this is wrong?

The problem is a rude parent will raise a rude child. It's almost genetic. Whole generations of rude people, raised by rude people, who have kids and raise more rude people. What are you going to do?

When it came time for my own children, I figured it was my job to help them learn how to behave. I learned the hard way—getting smacked. If I help them learn, maybe they'll grow up and teach their kids. So that's kind of genetic, too. I don't smack my kids, but I believe in being firm and teaching proper manners. I wish more parents did, too. One kid at a time, the world becomes a little more civilized.

Of course, not eating like a pig is pretty basic table manners. In order to do that, you might have to curb your appetite.

So here are some more Goomba Diet tips. These are weight-loss suggestions that can't possibly fail. You can cut out these foods without breaking a sweat, because no self-respecting goomba would ever eat any of this stuff anyway.

FOODS NOT ALLOWED ON THE GOOMBA DIET
- Your Irish *goomar's* cooking.
- Chocolate-covered ants.
- Spaghetti and matzoh balls.
- Garlic *naan*. Plus all other Indian food.
- Cup O Noodles.

Try giving up those foods for a month. That wasn't so hard, was it? You may not lose any weight, but it will sound good. You can tell your friends, "I've given up all pasta dishes except the ones that end in the letter *i*." Let them figure it out.

If this doesn't work for you, and you find yourself eating gigantic meals several times a day, and getting fat, you may need a more aggressive diet plan. Here's another Goomba Diet technique: Think about something that makes you lose your appetite. Is there a food you don't like eating? Think about that. Is there a person you don't like eating with? Think about that. Is there a place you hate to eat? Think about that.

If nothing's coming up for you, here are some other things to think about in order to stop thinking about food.

GOOMBA DIET MENTAL TECHNIQUES
- Think about having sex with your grandmother.
- Think about having sex with Laura Bush. Or Barbara Bush. Or Hillary Clinton.
- Think about having sex with George Bush. Either one of them.
- Think about having an intimate dinner date with Roseanne.

Now, sit down and try to eat a big meal.

If nothing you do curbs your appetite, you may be a guy who just has to eat too much. Maybe you have a slow metabolism. Maybe you have to eat exactly what you're eating. Three pizzas in one sitting? Who can say if that's too much? But if you find that you can't lose weight no matter how hard you try by altering your diet, here are some other techniques that might make you feel like you're losing weight—even if you're not.

GOOMBA DIET WEIGHT-LOSS SECRETS
- Hang around with goombas who are fatter than you.
- Empty your pockets.
- Wear extremely big clothes.
- Have your jaw wired shut. It worked for Michael Corleone.

As far as I'm concerned, every day is a special occasion. Be happy! Life is good! *Mangia!* In my family, we don't have to look very hard for something to celebrate.

My daughter had a music recital recently. She's just learning how to play the guitar, and this was her first performance. She had a little solo. She's been playing only a month, but already she has a little solo.

She's like me—she jumps in with both feet. She threw herself into studying the guitar, and when it was time for the solo, she went all out.

So naturally we had to celebrate. We went out for dinner afterward to—as usual—Il Cortile.

It was the usual eat-too-much meal. We did it right. We had prosciutto and some Parmesano-Reggiano—because my daughter loves that. We had some mozzarella and tomatoes. We had steamed clams in a red sauce. We had some baked clams.

Then we had dinner. Chicken parmigiana for some people, steaks for other people, penne à la vodka for everybody. I'm forgetting half of what we ate. It was a big dinner.

We're outside, afterward, trying to get a cab, and some broken-down guy in a broken-down limo comes rolling up and offers to take us home for $40. He's driving this gypsy cab with dents in the side and he wants $40.

It's not that far from Il Cortile to where I live. I wouldn't pay that much for a *new* limo.

It's not that I'm cheap. I'm generous. Even with limo drivers. A bunch of us from the show hired a limo recently. We were going to a wedding. It was me, Michael Imperioli, John Ventimiglia (who plays Artie Bucco on the show), Vince Curatola (who plays Johnny Sack), Dominic Chianese (who plays Uncle Junior), and some of our wives. It was like a *Sopranos* fun bus. We took the limo out to the wedding and we took it home. It was a flat rate of $500 for the night, and we tipped the guy another $250. That's generous, right?

But this guy with the gypsy limo, I told him no. Then he recognized me. Now he knows who I am, so he doesn't want to overcharge me. He dropped the price to $20. So I got into the most beat-up limo in New York City. My wife said it was almost embarrassing, like you wouldn't want to be seen by anyone you know, riding in that pile of junk. But, hey: It was winter. It was cold. It got us off the streets, and home.

And we were supposed to be celebrating. It was the end of another perfect Goomba Diet evening. I had eaten too much, maybe, and had a couple of glasses of wine, but it was a good meal, in a good restaurant, with family. Maybe we ate a few too many calories, but look at the big picture: What could be healthier than an evening like that?

CHAPTER 4

The Romantic Goomba

No goomba can be happy without love and romance in his life. He's not a loner. He's going to have a girlfriend, or he's going to have a wife. If he's got a wife, he might have a *goomar*, too—also known as a *goomada*—which is the mistress he sees on the sly. If he's got a wife and a *goomar*, he might even have a girlfriend on the side, too. Like with everything else, some goombas need more than others. If the goomba has a big appetite, he might have all three going at the same time.

But most of the goombas I know are married. They're family men. They married their high school sweethearts in their early twenties. Some of them are already "empty nesters," with their kids out of the house. A couple of them are already grandfathers!

That's not exactly my story. I knocked around a little while, and didn't get married until later. But it's really the goomba tradition: You get married young, and you stay married. Through thick and thin. No matter what.

There was a man on my block when I was a kid who had been married for fifty-eight years when his wife died. He was an old man by then. All he had left was the dog. When the dog died, that was the end. The old man died two weeks later.

There was my friend Carl, too. He was a fireman who died on 9/11. I knew him since kindergarten. He met his wife, Christine, when he was a kid. They were dating since he was twelve. He got her the ankle bracelet with her name on it, which no one wore on the ankle—you wore it on a chain around your neck—and then he got her the pre-engagement ring. Then the engagement ring. The engagement party. The showers. The wedding. Two wonderful kids.

You want to talk about a love affair? That's goomba romance. Christine is one of the great goomba-ettes, and Carl was a real, real family man—a goomba through and through.

And look at my own parents. My mother stayed with my father through two jail terms and even after he ran off with his *goomada*! I'm not saying it's right, but that's real goomba commitment. "For rich or for poor, in sickness and in health . . ." She was in it for the long haul.

That's goomba romance. And that's part of the Goomba Diet, too.

The goomba is only going to be eating and drinking for a certain amount of time every day. The rest of the time, what's he gonna do? He's gonna work and he's gonna be with his family. If he wants to be happy, he has to be as serious about his wife and children as he is about his lunch and dinner. He's got to devote himself to his family with the same enthusiasm he shows for his Sunday sauce.

Some guys don't know how to do this. They grew up in unhappy families, where nobody ever had a good time. So when they have their own families, they don't know how to have a good time themselves. Here are some ideas for appropriate and inappropriate goomba family activities.

GOOMBA FAMILY ACTIVITY DOS AND DON'TS

- Do play miniature golf. *Don't* play pocket pool.
- Do visit an ice cream parlor. *Don't* visit a massage parlor.
- Do rent *Deep Impact*. *Don't* rent *Deep Throat*.
- Do take the family to the beach. *Don't* take the family to a nude beach.
- Do take the kids for a drive. *Don't* take the kids for a *ride*.

When I was a kid, I didn't know too much about love and having a family. And I probably wasn't too interested in that, either. I remember going to certain movies and thinking, "What's the big deal?"

But I was very curious about sex. Even though it was a mystery to me, I could tell from what I heard that it was exciting and important.

I had my first girlfriend in the sixth grade. On graduation day, I took her to the movies. Me and two friends and our dates walked up 86th Street to Jan's Ice Cream Parlor. We were dressed in suits and the girls wore dresses. We had cheeseburger deluxes and sodas. Then we went to the movies.

I had no idea what I was doing, of course. No one had told me what to do. My mother taught me right from wrong. She taught me to be a good person.

But she never told me the dos and don'ts of dating. I never got no birds and bees story. I learned it out in the street.

That's where you went, in those days. You'd talk to an older guy on the block, or the pharmacist, or maybe your baseball coach. Guys would say, "How do you know if you got the clap?" or "What do you do if you think you got crabs?" Nobody went to their parents for that kind of thing, or to a doctor. You took that to the guys on the block.

One time, I remember, the older guys even set up a little goomba academy for a guy going on his first big date.

It was a Saturday afternoon in the early fall and the weather was still warm. We had all been at the park, playing football. We were dressed in jeans and T-shirts, and we went over to Bath Avenue and 16th, to the drugstore, to hang out on the corner.

The guy who had the big date coming up was nervous. He was really into this girl. He wanted to take her out to a nice place, but he'd never been to a nice place. He didn't know how to order, what wine to drink, or what.

So some of the guys dragged a table and two chairs out of the back of the drugstore and set them up right on the sidewalk. One of the older guys played the girl. Another one played the maître d'. Another one was the waiter. And they all acted out a night on the town.

They showed him how to behave—how to pull out the girl's chair, to stand up when she stands up, to put the napkin in your lap, how to order. They told him, "You order white wine if she's having fish, and red wine if she's having steak." They told him to order the house wine, unless he wanted to get really fancy and order something expensive, like Mateus. That's all we knew about wine.

They acted out the whole thing, until the guy was comfortable. Of course they were breaking his balls the whole time: "After she orders the wine, you ask if she would like to have a bite of your Italian sausage." But he got the lesson.

Some goombas have the same problem with sex that they have with food. They can't get enough. Once they get started, they can't stop. It's all they think about. They spend all their time and energy and money on sex.

Me and my true love, getting intimate.

Are you one of those goombas who can't get enough? Do you know a goomba who can't get enough? Here are some warning signs:

YOU MIGHT BE A SEX MANIAC IF . . .

- You've ever had sex on the dining room table. During Thanksgiving. At your grandmother's house.
- You enjoy a cigarette after sex. You're up to a carton a day.
- Your wife has a permanent limp. So does your *goomada*. So does her sister.

Somebody else's sex life is none of my business. But the sex-maniac approach is not the Goomba Diet approach. Just like eating too much makes you a pig, having sex too much makes you a pervert.

You have to decide for yourself. Obviously the goomba needs sex. Who doesn't? But how much is enough? How much is too much? When I was younger, I had all these questions. Is it bad to think about sex during school? During church? Is it bad to pay for sex? Is it bad to pay *too much* for sex? How much is too much?

Nowadays I'm not so confused. The answers are, in order, no, no, no, yes, and it depends. The "paying too much" question is a hard one. Last year I had a friend going to Las Vegas. He was interested in hookers. I didn't know what to tell him, so I got him to call my friend Frankie, who knows everything about everything. Frankie told him to get dressed real nice, go into a nice casino, and sit at the bar. Order a drink. Smile and look around. The girl will come to you. Get friendly, act like you're thinking about leaving. The girl will come on to *you*. She'll suggest going to your room. Tell her you're interested and ask how much. She will name a figure. It will seem very high—like, $1,000, or $1,500.

Don't panic. Act surprised. Say to the girl, "Really? That seems kinda high. I was here two months ago and I had a really nice time with a blonde girl named Mandy. It was three hundred bucks!"

The girl's price will fall immediately, probably to about $500. Then, Frankie said, you can make a decision about whether she's worth it.

It doesn't always work that way. I have a friend from New York who went out to Las Vegas for work. He called a guy I know and asked him to set him up with a girl. The guy introduced him to a very beautiful call girl. My friend asked the guy how much it was going to cost. The guy said, "Don't pay more than five hundred." But the girl asked for $1,000. She was so beautiful that my friend paid without hesitating—a thousand bucks, for a few hours with a call girl! I told my friend, "For me, for a thousand, she'd have to make it sing the national anthem."

If you're still not sure about the pervert thing, here are some other clues.

YOU MIGHT BE A SEX MANIAC IF . . .

- You're buying your condoms at Wal-Mart. By the crate.
- You have your own parking space at the adult book store.
- When you call the sex line, the girl that answers says, "Not *you* again."

When I was a teenager, some of the older guys I knew had girl-friends. They'd go on regular dates with them, and they'd bring them around for family dinners. On the weekends, they'd take them to these motels. The guys lived at home. The girls lived at home. If they were going to get any time together, they had to go someplace. So they'd drive out to these cheap motels.

Money was hard to come by for all of us in those days. Nobody was rolling in it. These guys were counting their pennies—even when it came to love and sex. I remember one of them saying there was a rule about getting a motel room: You had to come three times. If you didn't come three times, it wasn't worth the cost of the room.

Even though these were cheap motels, it was hard for most guys to scrape together the money for that kind of date. The motel rooms in Jersey cost $28. There was a Holiday Inn in Staten Island that was $49. If you weren't careful, with taxes and tips and every-thing, this could turn out to be a $75 or $100 night. That was a lot of money back then.

And it wasn't just the motel room. You needed to get a bottle of wine, or a six-pack of beer. You needed to get a bucket of fried chicken, or you'd pick up something to eat at Sbarro's—the orig-inal Sbarro's, before it was a big chain. The original Sbarro's was in Brooklyn, and Mama Sbarro herself worked there until just a few years ago. You'd get rice balls, prosciutto, mozzarella, roasted peppers, and maybe some *soopersat*—which was our name for the

Italian salami called soppressata. You'd take a bag of food with you.

One guy I knew had a system. He'd get a bucket of fried chicken and two six-packs of beer. He'd take his girl to the hotel. They'd have a few beers and maybe watch TV. Then they'd have sex. Then they'd eat. Maybe watch a little more TV. Then they'd have sex again. Then they'd sleep a little. Then they'd have sex, one last time, and leave. Three times! He got his money's worth.

Other guys I knew would split the cost. One guy would get the hotel room on a Friday at noon, say. He and his girl would have it from noon to six. He'd eat and drink and have sex. At six, he'd give the maid $3 and ask her to clean the room. Then he and his girl would go back to Brooklyn. He'd give the motel room key to a friend. The friend would go out a few hours later with his girl. Of course, neither girl would ever know about the arrangement. You wouldn't want her to think you were cheap.

In case you're just starting out, here are some tips on dating, goomba style.

GOOMBA DATING DOS AND DON'TS

DO: Take her to Atlantic City.
DON'T: Take her to Jersey City.

DO: Open the car door for her.
DON'T: Open it when the car is going 60 mph.

DO: Take her to visit the zoo.
DON'T: Take her to visit your Uncle Louie in the joint.

DO: Whisper romantic thoughts in her ear.
DON'T: Ask her if she'd like a bite of your braciole.

I wrote in my first book about how I got introduced to the actual mystery itself—the hot summer night, the golf course, the mosquito bites on my ass. After that, it was off to the races. I couldn't get enough.

I learned a lot from watching the older goombas in the neighborhood and listening to their stories. I'd see the guys going out or getting ready to go out. They had the tight-fitting slacks and the shirts open to the middle of the chest. They had the gold chains, and the horns, and maybe the cross. They had their hair cut one of two ways—either it was sort of feathered and parted in the middle, or it was combed straight back like the Fonz or those guys in the fifties. Anything else was unacceptable. A guy with a comb-over—*fugheddaboudit*. He didn't have a chance. These guys were wearing cologne. They had the Cadillac. And in their pockets was what we used to call the Jewish bankroll—a couple of hundred-dollar bills wrapped around a wad of singles.

The bankroll is essential. The goomba deals only in cash, as a rule. He likes to flash that wad around. He wants people to know he's got money. That's a way of showing people he's a big man. We're trained that way. My friend Kip remembers his Uncle Victor telling him, when he was a little boy, "When you got money in your pocket, you're a gentleman. When you don't, you're a bum."

If he was taking a girl out, especially if it was a first date, the goomba was going to an Italian restaurant. He was going to a place where they knew him—because he wanted to be treated like a big shot when he got there. He couldn't be a big shot if he was a stranger. So maybe he even went by the place the day before, tipped the maître d' or the waiters, and let them know he'd be coming back the next night. Remember, most of these guys were nobodies. They wouldn't have that phony bankroll if they weren't nobodies. But they couldn't let themselves be treated that way.

Either way, when the guy comes in with his date, the maître d' knows his name, and the waiter welcomes him like he's somebody important. This is even better if he takes the girl out of the neighborhood. Most of the girls we grew up with never left Brooklyn.

So if a guy takes his girl to Manhattan and gets this kind of treatment, the guy's like a king. It's like he's famous coast to coast.

The guy might order something special, like the osso bucco. He doesn't want to order chicken parm or lasagna. It's gotta be something he can't get at home. Then he's gotta order a bottle of wine. He might let the girl know how much it costs—and give her the cork, as a memento. This is an important evening. He's gotta keep reminding her of that.

After dinner, the goomba might take the girl to a show. If he's going to do it big, maybe he's going to get tickets for Tony Bennett or something. Maybe he hates Tony Bennett. Maybe he only likes the Bee Gees or ZZ Top. Doesn't matter. Tony Bennett is part of the goomba package—just like the pinky ring and the gold chain. It's part of the goomba accessory kit. He's already got the Tony Bennett tapes in the Cadillac, right next to the Sinatra, the Dean Martin, and the Barry White.

He's taking the girl to Tony Bennett, if he wants to make it happen.

Afterward, he's going to try to take the girl home or to a hotel. He's not taking her to a club, which is where he'd go if he was on his own. That's like taking sand to the beach—what for? He'd like to show off. He'd like the girl to see what a big shot he is at the club, how they welcome him at the door, and show him to the table, how every guy at the bar comes over to shake his hand.

But not tonight. Maybe that's for the second date.

Any other night, you always want to look like Tony Manero—the character played by John Travolta in *Saturday Night Fever*. Every time you come into the room, it's a big event. Everybody acts like they've been waiting all night for *you* to arrive. When you do, everybody's happy. Everybody shakes your hand. Everybody wants to order you a drink.

That's the goomba way. Never mind that the movie was just a movie, that it was based on a magazine article, and that the guy who wrote the magazine article later said he made it all up. It's the idea that counts. We all wanted to be Tony Manero.

I did my best. I wore the clothes. I bought the shoes. I got the haircut. I learned the dance moves. I was about as smooth as you would expect. And I got a little action.

I was never a pig about it, though. I went out as much as the other guys. I was better looking and skinnier than I am now. I never lied or cheated to get laid, or anything like that. I didn't have to. I got my share, and I had a lot of laughs.

When I moved to Las Vegas, it was different. Everybody was going out with everybody. You never saw so much sex. Any half-decent guy could have gone with a different girl every single night of the week, just by being half decent. It was incredible. Between the cocktail waitresses and the dancers and the strippers and the hookers, it was wall-to-wall sex. Some guys went a little nuts.

There were hookers who, when they were off-duty, would date like regular girls. I knew guys who went out with them. This was weird to me at first. Before I got to Vegas, I thought the only girls who were hookers either walked the streets or worked in those whorehouses in New York. They were girls who did blow jobs in the back of the car for $5, or girls you'd see hanging around in the dark corners in Coney Island. But these girls in Vegas were just like the other girls—the cocktail waitresses, the bartenders, the dealers— who worked the other jobs. They just happened to be hookers.

There were call girls, too, who were the same thing only a little more expensive and a little classier. Not much, but a little. At three o'clock, they were off-duty, just like the rest of us. Some of them were so pretty, you couldn't tell they were working girls. You'd think they were tourists or maybe dancers or something. Then you'd find out. I always thought it was a little strange, to think about what they did for a living. I remember going out with this girl who was so beautiful that I couldn't believe she was a hooker. But I knew she was, and it bothered me. She said, "What's wrong? Don't you like me?" I just couldn't stop thinking that she'd already been with five or six guys that night, and that I was going to be next. I wasn't going to be paying for it, and I knew she liked me, but still . . . I wasn't going for that.

You gotta draw the line somewhere, right? But some of the guys I knew went overboard. It was sex, all the time sex.

Me, I just had a good time. I went around with a lot of girls. But I never did anything I'd have to be ashamed of. That's because I had a sort of code. My friend Charles Najjar said to me one time, "Never hit on a girl who doesn't like you." That was my rule. If a girl didn't give me some kind of signal, I wouldn't pursue her. She had to show me something. I wasn't going to like a girl who didn't like me. You wouldn't be able to meet girls who would say, "Steve was an asshole." I was always a nice guy.

I knew guys who would say anything, or do anything, to get laid. I had one friend who would just go up to every girl he met and ask her, right away, if she wanted to come back to his place. He'd say to me, "Hey, I'm just playing the percentages. *Somebody's* gonna say yes."

Other guys had standards that were too high—at the beginning of the evening, at least. They'd say, "She's too young," or "She's so skinny." Then, at the end of the night, they'd wind up with whoever was left. They'd stick around until the last minute and go home with whoever they could.

Sometimes, it was desperate. There's this guy I know who told me a story about picking up two broads one night with his cousin. The girls wanted to get some cocaine. This guy and his cousin didn't have any cocaine, but they had some quaaludes. The cousin says, "Excuse me," and goes out to the car. The guy hears this terrible banging sound. He looks out the window. His cousin has the trunk of the car open and he's smashing something with a tire iron. He comes back a few minutes later and says, "Here you are, ladies!" So the girls end up snorting smashed quaaludes, thinking it was cocaine.

That's two sick guys.

I never had to lower myself to that. I never got that desperate or that sick.

Sex was everywhere in those days. Remember, this was before AIDS and after the Pill. You weren't that worried about getting a girl pregnant and you weren't worried at all about catching a disease that would kill you. It was all a lot more innocent than it is today.

There was a guy I delivered pizzas with who had sex with one of his customers. One night he delivered a medium pepperoni pizza and a six-pack of Coke to this woman. She invited him in. The next thing he knows they're having sex. It was like getting a really good tip.

The next week, she called and ordered another medium pepperoni pizza with a six-pack of Coke. He went back and the same thing happened. He delivered the pizza and then they went to bed.

This went on for quite a while. She'd call and place the order and he'd make the delivery. Then one night she called and said, "By the way, would you stop at the store on your way over? I'm out of orange juice."

That was it. My friend said, "If that's what I was looking for, I'd get married." He refused to make the delivery.

I guess he wasn't as desperate as some guys I know. They're not put off by anything.

I have one friend, whose name I won't use, who goes down to the Caribbean to this sex resort. They have girls there. You check in, and you have sex. That's all you do. There's no golf. There's no tennis. There's no snorkeling. It's just sex.

My friend calls it a "whore hotel." The first time he went, he flew down for five days. He stayed three weeks. He couldn't get enough. The second time he went down, he stayed for ten days. He knew he had gone overboard when he ran out of condoms, after ten days. He had brought thirty condoms.

The girls cost $30 for a couple of hours or $60 for the whole night. They're local girls and they get checked once a month—which, given the mileage on these broads, you have to wonder is that often enough? They come to the hotel and stand around until someone picks them. The time my friend stayed twenty-one days, he went with eighteen different girls—because he saw some of the same girls twice. Some of them were so good, he said, he couldn't help going back for seconds.

Every afternoon there would be a shift change. The new girls would show up. There'd be forty or more of them, hanging around at the bar by the pool. (The first time my friend went, they gave him a room on the second floor. No good, my friend said: He had to have something on the *first* floor, next to the bar, so he could get first crack at the new arrivals.) The guests were all guys like him, Americans and Europeans. Mostly they come in groups of two or three. Some of them are bachelor parties. Some of them are on business trips. Guys eat together, or hang out in the Jacuzzi together, in between the time they spend with the girls. The place is owned by an American guy.

For my friend, this is the perfect vacation. He's been back three or four times.

The rooms cost $45. A big dinner was $60, with booze. Without using a calculator, I'm going to guess my friend was spending about $200 to $300 a day—once you figure in incidentals and tips. So that's about $5,000 or so for the twenty-one days. That's a lot of money, just to get laid.

Is that too much? It's not for me to say. I mean, I like to get laid as much as the next guy, but I like to do other stuff, too.

What kind of souvenirs do you bring back from a vacation like that? How do you explain twenty-one days in the Caribbean and no suntan?

All the basic rules of dating apply to every goomba, no matter his age or situation. Remember that dating sometimes leads to marriage. The girl you're taking out on Friday night—she could be the one! You could have children with this woman—and even grandchildren. So be smart. Be careful. Watch your mouth. Try to be a gentleman. You may think you're just trying to get a piece of ass, but you should treat it as something more important than going out to get a slice of pizza. Here are some final suggestions for successful dating.

GOOMBA RULES FOR DATING

- Never get too serious about a woman you haven't slept with. She could be hiding something from you–like a penis.
- Never use olive oil as a sexual lubricant. This is a waste of olive oil. Use something cheap that you can't eat, like Vaseline.
- Never get carried away on the first date. Remember, no matter how hot you think she is, there's somebody, somewhere, who's already sick and tired of her.
- Never disrespect a woman you're dating. Remember, no matter how nuts you think she is, she might be the woman you end up marrying.

CHAPTER 5

La Famiglia

Love is a big part of the Goomba Diet. And love means more than just dating and sex. Love means *famiglia*—the family you're born into, and the family you make.

It's all part of keeping the goomba happy. A goomba who has no love is an unhappy goomba. What's an unhappy goomba going to do? He's going to eat too much. He eats too much, he gets too fat and—there you go. He's going to need one of those other diets where you actually have to stop eating.

Nobody wants that to happen.

Like I said, the goomba is a family man. He grows up in a house full of people—sisters, brothers, parents, grandparents, and even more. So when he starts a family, he's probably going to start a big one.

Most of the guys I know today were surrounded by big families like that when they were younger. Stevie Van Zandt grew up in Boston, in an Italian family, living in the same house with his grandparents. His mother's father was the patriarch of the clan. Even when his mother remarried a non-Italian and moved to New Jersey, they moved the grandparents, too. "My father became an honorary Italian, and we were a regular Italian family—but it was all happening in this microcosm in the New Jersey suburbs. We were the only Italians for miles around."

Michael Imperioli's childhood was more traditional. When he was a kid in Mt. Vernon, New York, his grandparents lived on the ground floor and his family lived on the second floor. His grandfather was Sicilian and he insisted on eating at home. He loved his wife's cooking, plus he didn't trust restaurants, even Italian restaurants. He thought they were charging too much, and that there probably weren't even real Italians in the kitchen.

My *Sopranos* colleague Lorraine Bracco had a similar background, but with a little twist. Her mother was from England—a "war bride" married to her Italian father when he was serving overseas.

The Italian side of Lorraine's family was from Palermo. In her house, in the Bay Ridge section of Brooklyn, Sunday dinner always included her grandmother, her great-grandmother, her aunts, her uncles, and her cousins, and her own brother and sister. "We didn't live with all of them, but we ate with all of them. Sometimes we were fifty people for dinner." In her grandmother's apartment. The meal always included macaroni, a meat dish, some risotto, and ricotta balls.

So for pretty much all of us, Sunday dinner was a madhouse, a giant table of the whole family, everyone eating and drinking and talking at once. If you weren't used to it, it would probably drive you crazy. If you grew up that way, it seemed normal.

Some goombas love family so much they have more than one. I know men who've got two or three of them—current wives, current *goomars,* ex-wives, ex-*goomars.* The goomba loves children so much that he might even have children with all of these.

This isn't true of most goombas. The average goomba has one wife, the original one, and a few kids. Most of them are overachievers in the kid department. They got four or five, where I have only two. Most of them come from big families, like I do, and most of their brothers and sisters have lots of kids, too. Both of their parents came from big families, and the aunts and uncles also have lots of kids. A family reunion is like a convention. You gotta book a catering hall just to get everybody in the same room.

Obviously it starts with the marriage. The goomba's got to get a wife. Most of the goombas I know married girls from the neighborhood, or girls who could have been from the neighborhood only they grew up somewhere else. They're Italian and they're from Brooklyn or Jersey. They're Catholic. Their parents were hard-working people. They came from big families, and they're interested in having big families. They know how to cook the goomba food and live the goomba life.

Some of them are real goomba-ettes. They've got the nails and the hair and the pants and the tan, and as usual with the goomba-ettes, they overdo everything. You see them at Ravioli Fair or Spumoni Gardens. The nails are out to here and the hair is as soft as a bowling ball. The pants are too tight. The voice is too loud. Their tan is ridiculous. It looks like Kentucky Fried Chicken—extra crispy.

Don't get me wrong. I *love* the goomba-ette. She's tough and she's loyal and she's strong, and she makes a good wife and a good mother and a great friend. Some of the best broads I know are the goomba-ettes who are married to guys I grew up with. They're the kind of people you could turn to in any kind of emergency and know they'd be there. No questions asked, no matter what. If I had stayed in the neighborhood, I probably would have married one.

My life took a different turn. I went to Las Vegas. I got lucky. I married Laura.

I knew when I met her that she was something special. She was working as a cocktail waitress. Some lady was bugging her. So Laura said, "Why don't you go fuck yourself?"

The lady said, "I beg your pardon?"

Laura said, "Go. Fuck. Yourself."

My wife, Laura, and me, back in the day.

I knew that was the woman for me.

Laura's not Italian. She's not a goomba-ette. But she's got a lot of the qualities that I admire in the goomba-ette. She's totally loyal. I know she's got my back. Some WASPy broads, when the well runs dry, you know they're gonna run out on you. That's not for me.

Laura knew me when I had no money. She had my back then, too. Later, when I hated my job in Las Vegas, even though I was making good money, she told me to try something different. She looked me right in the eye and said, "Quit. If I have to, I'll go out and get a job. I can't stand seeing you unhappy like this."

Nothing has changed. These days I'm doing all right, and she's still got my back.

In my marriage, we stay out of each other's way a lot. I got my stuff. Laura's got her stuff. She's not one of those wives who meddle. She doesn't call my agent or my manager and yell at them for not getting me some part in a movie. She goes out with her mom or her friends. I do my work or go out with my friends. When we're together, we're together all the way. But we give each other some space. Some couples I know, they can't bear to be apart. They're with each other twenty-four hours a day. I'm not saying that's wrong. But it's not for me.

The secret to a happy marriage is . . .

Who am I kidding? There is no secret to a happy marriage. There's a *hundred* secrets to a happy marriage. Ask any guy who's been married to the same woman for more than a couple of years and he'll tell you his secret. One guy I know says, "Lie! Lie about everything." Another guy I know says, "Just say yes. Whatever she wants, just say yes. Do what you have to do. But never disagree." Another guy I know says, "Dummy up, dummy up, dummy up. Whatever she says, you don't know. Never look at another girl. If she says, 'Do you think she's pretty?' you say, 'Who?' Dummy up."

Those techniques are all right—for them. Me, I think the secret is to be loving, to be considerate, to try and treat your wife the way you did when she was just your girlfriend and you were *hoping* she would be your wife. Send her flowers. Remember your anniversary and her birthday. Take her out to dinner someplace nice once in a while, without the kids. Share your problems with her. Find out what she's going through.

That's pretty simple stuff, but it works for me.

There are certain problems that are bound to come up in any marriage. You can start working on the solution now. You can practice saying, "A big ass hasn't hurt Jennifer Lopez's career," or "Have another cannoli—you could stand to put on a pound or two." You can practice lines like, "Sure, your mother can stay here for a month," or "I think you *deserve* more jewelry."

In case it's too confusing, here are some tips for preventing your current or future wife from becoming your future ex-wife.

GOOMBA TIPS FOR A HAPPY MARRIAGE

DO: Tell her, "Of course you should try a Brazilian wax."
DON'T: Tell her, "Do the mustache, too."

DO: Try to become more intimate with her.
DON'T: Wake her up and make her have sex with you.

DO: Tell her she's a great cook.
DON'T: Ask her if she actually *cooked* the macaroni before serving it.

DO: Compliment her meatballs.
DON'T: Say, "You could serve these with a tennis racquet."

DO: Compliment her in bed.
DON'T: Ask her, "Do you know how much a hooker charges
to do that?"

DO: Offer to feed the baby.
DON'T: Offer to have your *goomada* breast-feed the baby.

DO: Tell her, "I dreamed about you last night."
DON'T: Tell her, "I dreamed you could actually *cook*."

GOOMBA PARENTING

Probably most people don't think of the goomba as a real family
man, or as a serious father. Their idea of the goomba is Tony
Soprano or Vito Corleone, tough guys who got no business even
talking about being parents.

But that's the movies and TV. In real life, most of the goombas
I know are right in there. That's because they're goombas. They're
big-hearted guys by nature. They might not like the idea of chang-
ing a dirty diaper—I've changed more than a few, believe me, and
there's nothing about it that I like—but from the minute they set
eyes on their first-born child, *fugheddaboudit*. They're in.

That's what happened to me. Being a father is the most important thing in my life. Being a father has been more complicated,
more exciting, more aggravating, more gratifying, and more confusing than anything I've ever done before. It's full of surprises. I
never know what's coming next, which is part of the joy of it.

I would rather spend time with my wife and kids than anyone
else on the planet. They're smart and funny and they're interested
in everything. They're also independent and headstrong. They see
me on TV, but I'm still just their father. They love and respect me,
but as far as being a TV star, they ain't impressed.

Like every other first-time father, in the beginning I had no one
to guide me. My own father had been a washout in the parenting
department. I coulda used a book like this to show me what to

expect and how to behave. I don't know if I would have read the part on being a parent, because I didn't know how complicated it was going to be. You don't know what you don't know, and I had no idea what I was in for.

Most goomba dads think all you gotta do is bring the baby home from the hospital and hang a provolone over the crib and bing! They're done. They think when you run out of diapers you can just cut down one of Uncle Zito's Depends. They think getting a baby's shoes bronzed is basically the same thing those guys did when they fitted Sallie Tomatoes with cement overshoes. They got no clue.

The goomba-ette wife is a little better prepared. She already knows there's going to be vomit and diarrhea and urine-soaked pants—'cause she's married to a slob goomba! She has to expect the baby to make this kind of mess, too.

So here's a little guidance—a primer for the first-time goomba father and a refresher course for the goomba veteran.

GOOMBA PARENTING DOS AND DON'TS

DO: Try to make the baby burp.
DON'T: Try to make the baby fart.

DO: Have the baby circumcised.
DON'T: Do it yourself with your cigar cutter.

DO: Take pictures of your new child.
DON'T: Make them all look like mug shots.

There's more to it than that. Being a parent is hard. It's a full-time job. Most people don't do it very well. Since you don't have to register or get a license or a permit before you try it—unlike voting, driving, owning a gun, owning a car, or anything else important—lots of people become parents without having any information about parenting or any real interest in doing the job.

This is one of my pet peeves. Where I live now, every time I take a walk, I see a woman walking on the street or in the park with her Jamaican nanny pushing her kid in the stroller. Not the Jamaican nanny's kid—the white lady's kid. This makes me crazy. I want to go up to the lady and say, "Are you that child's mother? Then *act* like the child's mother!"

I know there are lots of parents who need help. There's single mothers who need a lot of help. They need a nanny to come in and watch the kid while they go to work, or go shopping, or whatever. In Vegas, where I used to live, they have twenty-four-hour nurseries and preschools—so the mom can drop the kid off on her way to her job at the casino. You got kids working the graveyard shift just like their parents!

But who needs a nanny to go to the park with them and push their kid in the stroller or on the swings? For what? So they can talk on their cell phones? It ain't right.

And it isn't just the park. The nanny drops the kid off at school in the morning, which I know because I'm dropping off *my* daughters at school in the morning, and the nanny picks the kid up at school in the afternoon, which I know because I'm picking up *my* daughters at school in the afternoon. The nanny goes home and does homework with the kid and then they go down to the park to play, which I know because I'm taking *my* kids down to the park to play.

Then, at night, the parents come home and they go *out*—without their kids—which I know because my wife and I are leaving the building, with our kids, on our way out to dinner.

Why have kids at all? For the tax break?

It's a yuppie thing. It's like an accessory. It's like having an SUV. You get one of those four-wheel-drive monsters with the snow tires not because you're going to be driving up the side of some frozen mountain but because all your friends have one and you want one, too. You shop at Bergdorf Goodman and Barneys and you drive a Mercedes SUV. And you have a Jamaican nanny push your designer kid in his designer baby clothes and his designer stroller because you're too busy to do it yourself.

I think it's bullshit. I got nothing in the world against Jamaicans, but if I wanted my kid raised by a Jamaican woman, I would have married a Jamaican woman and moved to Kingston.

I spend time with my kids. I care about my kids. I think being with them is important. And I think that if you're going to be a parent, you better act like you're serious about it. If you're lucky enough to have kids—and a lot of people who would die to have children can't—then you'd better enjoy it.

Don't get me started.

A big part of the Goomba Diet is being fulfilled in everything you do. But even if your heart's in it, being a parent is a hard job. So here's some more tips on being a good goomba parent.

MORE GOOMBA PARENTING DOS AND DON'TS

DO: Encourage your daughters to play sports.
DON'T: Make Jell-O wrestling one of the sports.

DO: Give your kids an allowance.
DON'T: Offer to make it double or nothing by shooting craps.

DO: Tell your son about the facts of life
DON'T: Do this by taking him to House of Lee Oriental Massage.

The center of the goomba family is the Sunday dinner. This is like going to church for Catholics or going to temple for Jews, except that it's not optional. It isn't only for observant goombas. It's for all goombas. You *all*, the whole goomba family tribe, gather on Sunday for the weekly dinner.

When I was a kid it was crazy. It was aunts and uncles and cousins all together. These ones would be fighting. These ones would not be speaking to each other. These ones would be arguing. And everybody would be cooking and eating.

Is this a beautiful picture or what?

The day starts very early. The cook is going to do a lot of shopping for the day. She's going to get nothing but the best. So she doesn't just get in the minivan and drive to Best Foods. She gets her little trolley and she walks down the street. She stops at the pork store for one cut of meat and the butcher for another—sausages in one place, steaks in the other. She goes to the fish store for her clams and shrimp and lobster. She goes to the green grocer for her fruits and vegetables. She goes to the cheese store for her fresh Parmesan and the mozzarella. (You will never see a goomba use the Parmesan that you shake out of those green cans. This would be death in a goomba family. And you never see a goomba buy those bags of mozzarella that are already grated. This would be illegal in a goomba family.) She goes to the bakery for her cannoli. Then, and only then, she goes to the actual supermarket—to get the other stuff that it doesn't matter where you buy. She gets her olive oil and her canned tomatoes and her butter and so on at the supermarket.

When I was a kid, my grandmother did this sort of thing during the week, too, because she worked as a cook. She used to make Italian dinners that could be frozen and sold later, for the neighborhood deli. She'd make lasagna and baked ziti and cannelloni and manicotti, and the deli would freeze it and slap a sticker on it and sell it to the people in the neighborhood. Everyone knew my grandmother's cooking, and her house was always full of the smell of cheese and marinara sauce. Many's the day I spent helping her grate the cheese or stir the sauce.

On Sunday morning, the principal cook in the house, whether it's the mother or the grandmother, is already cooking before the man of the house has had his morning coffee. She's making meatballs. She's cooking Sunday sauce. She's roasting ribs. She's stuffing ravioli. She's baking bread. The kitchen looks like World War Three already, and it isn't even nine o'clock.

By noon, everything is under control. Most of the food is cooked or cooking. The goomba dad has probably been able to get into the kitchen for a little breakfast. Lunch is going to be a pretty light affair, now. He's going to watch the game on TV. Maybe a few friends are coming over to help him with that. They're going to drink a beer or two, sit in front of the TV in their sweat suits, maybe smoke a cigar and talk sports. This is a men-only thing. The wives don't come over for this or, if they do, they go into the kitchen and drink coffee and talk about whatever wives talk about. The guys watch the game and scratch themselves and fart and act like guys. And eat snacks. They don't dare try to get a piece of whatever's coming for dinner, which they can smell cooking while they watch the game. But they might get offered a meatball, or a little plate of sausage and peppers, or a rice ball. Maybe they'll get a slice of prosciutto and mozzarella, or some fried meatballs. If the cook is big-hearted, she might even make a sandwich or two.

But the goomba stays out of the kitchen. For the most part, there's not that many Molto Marios around. The goomba family is an old-fashioned family. The father is in the living room or the den watching the game. The mother is in the kitchen rattling the pots and pans. Just like their parents did.

By about three o'clock the game is over and the guys are leaving and the guests are starting to arrive. Here's Uncle Aldo and Auntie Mary. Here's cousin Jimmy and his wife, Karen. Here's your brother Tony and his second wife, Angela, and their three kids. Here's your wife's sister Carol, and her husband, Frankie, and their three kids. Before you know what's happening, the house is full of family. There's not enough chairs and sofas for everyone to sit on, so you sit down for dinner instead.

The meal is huge, and the food is amazing, starting with the soup and ending with the dessert. It takes two hours to eat it, and four bottles of wine, and four bottles of Pellegrino. All of the guys have undone their belts and the top buttons of their pants—they have to, or they'll die. The kids have gotten bored and been excused from the table.

All of the family business has been discussed. All the dirty laundry has come out. If you didn't know before, now you know who's pregnant, who's getting married, who's getting a divorce, who's going to have a goiter removed, who's selling his house, who's getting fired from his job, and who's going to prison. Because the family is so big, and the extended family is so much bigger, even though you never met your wife's cousin's niece Cynthia, you're still going to hear how her husband had a nervous breakdown and ran off with some Korean massage parlor girl. Which causes at least one of the women at the table to cross herself and stare at her husband and say, "I swear, Carlo, if you *ever* . . ."

It's exhausting. By the time it's over, after the coffee and the Sambuca and the dessert have been cleared away, the goomba is beat. He's had a full day. This is the highlight of the week for him. He's hardly got the energy to get to bed. But it's Sunday night, and tomorrow's Monday, and most goombas have to get up and get the new week started first thing in the morning. So maybe he's going to turn on HBO and watch a little TV before he drops off to sleep.

Where he has a nightmare about a Korean massage parlor girl.

Not everyone loves the Sunday dinner like I do. My friend Vince Curatola grew up in a typical goomba family in Bergen

My good friends Maureen and Vince, with Laura, at Rao's.

County—in Englewood, New Jersey. He lived with his brother and his mom and dad, and also with his grandmother and grandfather. It was real Italian-American. His mother came from Sicily but spoke English like a native. His father was from Calabria. His grandmother had been trained as a cook, when she was a teenager, working in a place that catered to celebrities like Mayor Fiorello LaGuardia and the opera star Enrico Caruso. So she knew her way around the kitchen.

Every Sunday was a huge celebration. There would be thirty people in the house if it was just family. And it was never just family. Vince's father was a successful masonry contractor, and the neighborhood they lived in was popular with celebrities. Vince remembers family dinners where people at the table included Tony Bennett, who had a house on the same street, and Ezio Pinza—the Metropolitan Opera star who sang "Some Enchanted Evening" to Mary Martin who was in *South Pacific* on Broadway.

Ask him now and he says, "I had enough of that when I was a kid—all that 'automatic company' where the house is full all the time. My idea of a nice Sunday now is a quiet dinner with my wife. Unless I'm out with my friends, I'd rather be home alone with my wife. But not everyone is like that. I wish I had ten cents for every person who's ever come up to me and told me how they love to invite everyone over for a huge Sunday meal and then watch *The Sopranos*. I'd be rich."

The lucky goomba who's a father is going to look forward to being a grandfather. This is a position of great respect in all goomba families. The grandfather is the king. He's the wise one, the godfather. Everyone will show him respect.

Most goombas have no clue how to be fathers until they're fathers. They have no clue how to be grandfathers, either. They might have had a grandfather or two, but they probably weren't paying attention at the time. They could have been studying how to be a good grandfather. But when you're young, you never think about these things.

You can identify the goomba grandfathers in any crowd. Here are some tell-tale signs:

YOU'RE A GOOMBA GRANDFATHER IF . . .

- You always offer your grandson seconds at the table. And thirds, and fourths, and fifths, and sixths, . . .
- Your grandson has a permanent bruise on his cheek from you pinching him.
- You have so many pictures of your grandchildren on the front of your refrigerator that you can't actually see the refrigerator.
- You've already bought your grandson a baseball mitt, a hockey stick, a football helmet, and a soccer ball. He's seven months old.

I know from experience that you don't fool around with a goomba's grandkids, any more than you make jokes about his mother or his wife. A goomba might complain about his own children. A lot of goombas do that. This one won't get a job. This one's in a bad marriage. This one will never get into college.

You never hear a goomba complain about his grandchildren. If you make the mistake of asking a goomba grandfather about his grandson's weight problem, he's going to say, "What weight problem?" and then smack you in the head. You've seen the kid. He wears bigger pants than you do. The kid's breasts are larger than your *goomar's*. He looks like Jackie Gleason.

The only thing you're allowed to say about a boy like that is, "Good-looking kid." Don't even think about adding, "He's got his mother's tits."

When I was a kid, grandparents were old people. They lived like old people. In their apartments, you couldn't even see the furniture because of the plastic covers. The sofa was invisible. There were more crosses on the wall than they have in most cemeteries. There were more pictures of Jesus on the wall than you see in a church. If the TV was on, it was showing Lawrence Welk. The grandfather wore a hat and a suit, always, except when he was gardening, in which case he took off his jacket and just had the shirt and tie. The grandmother wore a dress and stockings and nice shoes, always, except when she was cooking, in which case she also wore an apron. They both wore dark colors. They both stayed home a lot. They usually lived in the basement apartment of the house. Their children lived on the upper floor. Everyone shared the middle floor. The only time you saw them out in the street, unless they were your own grandparents, was on the front stoop. This is where they did their socializing. Sometimes you'd see them at a wedding or a funeral. Sometimes the grandfather would go play bocce ball in the park, or sit and drink an espresso with his friends. Sometimes the grandmother would have her friends over for coffee and cake.

Nowadays, it's all different. People are living longer. They're living *larger*. Old people think they're young when they're not young. I know seventy-year-old guys, guys who have grandchildren, who live like my grandfather did when he was forty. They got *goomadas*. They still bounce around at night. They drive expensive cars and have nice jewelry and nice clothes. You see them on the corner, in their sweat suits and their gold chains, smoking cigarettes outside the social club, calling their bookies, laying down bets. On the weekends you sometimes see them out with the girlfriends. They still drink. They still smoke cigars. They still go to the track. Some of them still *dance*.

I heard a story about some old guys last year. They were arrested for bookmaking and loan sharking and money laundering. There were about ten of them, and they were all over seventy! It was like *The Godfather* meets *The Grandfather*.

Not that I think being a criminal's a good career move at any age, but these guys are still very active. I think it's great. It gives me hope. It's going to be a lot of years before I'm ready for grandchildren, but I hope I'm still bouncing around like that when they get here.

I'm a lucky guy. I love my kids—all dads love their kids—but I also *like* my kids. I like being around my kids. I understand that's not true for some parents. I hear guys say things like, "My kids are out of school for the summer and they're driving me crazy." I'm sorry for them. I love it when my kids are out of school for the summer.

I like having them close to me. Most goombas feel that way. So they don't get all carried away with the summer-camp thing like a lot of WASP families and Jewish families that I know. Those people send their kids away to camp. The kids go every summer. When they're old enough, they go and work as counselors. You hear them talk about how they spent every summer of their childhood up at Camp Runnamucka, and it was the greatest thing that ever happened to them.

Not in my family. My wife refuses to even consider it. Our daughters, away from us, all day and all night, in the middle of the summer, for eight weeks? Are you crazy? My wife says she couldn't even imagine it. I agree. I'd miss them too much.

Beauties and the beast: Me and my girls.

Day camp, sure. I did that when I was a kid. And I went to sleepaway camp, a couple of summers. My dad wasn't around, and my mother wanted us to be someplace outside the city where it was nice, so I went away to Camp IBG—for Italian Board of Guardians. There was a priest in charge. I went for two weeks. It was mostly Italian kids like me. The only difference was that most of the other kids paid. We didn't have the money. Somehow my mother wangled a deal, though, for me and my two sisters. One summer, when my mother was in the hospital for gallbladder surgery, I went twice—once for two weeks with the eight-to-twelve-year-olds, and then again for the second session with the older kids. I was about nine. I was homesick as hell, too, but the next time I went, I liked it.

Given my options, then, summer camp wasn't so bad. But now, for my kids, no thanks. I don't want them to be away from me for that long.

Most of the goombas like having a lot of family around on holidays, too. I went to a Fourth of July party recently. It was a bunch of guys from the neighborhood, and they all brought their kids. There were cousins and aunts and uncles and grandparents. It was like a junior goomba training seminar. The kids were playing football, dodgeball, Wiffle ball, for hours. The parents were drinking wine, drinking martinis, talking. And there was a cookout that went on for hours—steaks, sausages, chicken, hot dogs . . . I loved it. I love being around the kids.

In the old days you used to be able to buy fireworks for your Fourth of July. We'd go down to Chinatown and buy all these M-80s and Ashcans, and things with names like the Moon Shot and the Sizzler. We'd sit out and fire everything off once it got dark. No more. I guess it's not safe anymore.

We went to a graduation party last June for my friend Puddy's son. He's my godson and I've known this kid literally since he was born, and now he's graduating from high school. He's going off to college, so his family threw him a big party to celebrate.

It was a good old-fashioned graduation party, like from the old days. We had stuffed eggplant with ricotta, sausage and peppers, penne with marinara sauce, fettucine with Alfredo sauce, ribs, roast pork, broccoli rabe, hot dogs for the kids, nice Italian bread, a big Caesar salad . . . you name it. There was so much food! I'm forgetting half of what was there.

The guest list was just family and friends—but that's seventy-five people. The kid's aunts and uncles were there, and grandparents, and the cousins, plus families like mine, and our kids. It was held in the backyard under a tent. There was a lot of wine and a lot of laughter and a lot of happiness for this kid. He's going off to a music college, so naturally the celebration ended with music—a concert in the basement. Puddy's son is on drums, another son is on bass, their sister is on keyboard. It was like the Goomba Partridge family.

I love all that stuff.

But there's guys who don't. Every once in a while I'll meet some family where the kids' last name isn't the same as the father's last name. What happens is a man and woman get married, have kids, and then the marriage falls apart. Okay. That happens. Then the woman remarries, and the kids get adopted or whatever by the new stepdad.

I don't go with that. I think the lowest thing a guy can do is give up his name, and let some other person start being the father to his children. Not that there's anything wrong with stepdads. I know some good stepdads. I don't think there's anything wrong with people going through a divorce, if they're that unhappy, or with getting married again later. But when a guy gives up his kids . . .

The goomba ain't going for that.

I had a friend whose sister was married to a degenerate gambler. He was a big noisy guy around town—very flashy, big businessman—who gave her this huge ring. They got married and went to Las Vegas for the honeymoon. They check into the hotel and go up to the room, and the guy excuses himself for a minute.

She never saw him again for the rest of the honeymoon. He was gambling—all day, all night. She's in the room waiting, and he's down in the casino gambling. He blew everything they had—all the money from the *a boost,* all the honeymoon money, everything they brought with them is gone.

He loses $30,000—and this was back when that was a lot of money. When they get home, they're broke. She doesn't know how she's going to pay the mortgage, so she decides to hock the ring.

It's a phony. It's cubic zirconium. Everything about this guy was a lie.

She manages to pay the mortgage. Then she finds out she's pregnant. This guy continues to be a degenerate, even after the child is born. He doesn't straighten out. In fact, he gets worse.

The woman is a wreck. Her life is ruined. She turns to her father. So he makes an offer to the guy, behind his daughter's back. He tells the guy he'll give him $25,000 cash, but he wants the guy to give up the child and disappear, and never come around again.

The guy was still a degenerate, so of course he took the offer. He took the money and he left. The family was better for it.

But to me that's the lowest of the low. I can't imagine anything worse.

I think kids strengthen a marriage. They give you something to talk about, something to worry about, something to share an interest in. You gotta do something to keep a marriage alive. I mean, after fifteen or twenty years together, what else is there to talk about? How many dinners can you go out to? How many mornings can you look at each other across the breakfast table?

With my wife, there's always something new and something interesting to discuss, and it usually involves the kids. So it never gets old.

Some goombas, to be honest, have another way to keep the marriage from getting old. They have a *goomar*—the traditional, old-fashioned goomba girlfriend.

I'm not saying it's right. I'm not saying I recommend it. It certainly isn't my thing. But it's real and there's a lot of it going around. Many's the goomba who's got a little something, or a lot of something, on the side.

The *goomar* is the weekend girlfriend, like a mistress, who the goomba sees when he's not with his family. Sometimes he's just as faithful to the *goomar* as he is to the wife. He might have both, but he's not cheating on them. He might have been with the *goomar* just as long as he's been with the wife. Or longer. I know a goomba who started seeing the *goomar* even before he knew his wife. He couldn't marry the girlfriend, for some reason, but he couldn't stop seeing her, either. So they continued as boyfriend and girlfriend, even though he got married and had kids someplace along the line.

Part of what makes the whole *goomada* thing exciting is that it's a secret. Well, sort of a secret. Most guys, if they have one, all their friends know they have one, since goombas don't like to do anything alone. In fact, most goombas who have *goomars* will go out every once in a while with the other guys who have *goomars*. You never go anyplace with her where you go with your wife, of course, because that would be disrespectful. But your friends will know who the *goomar* is. One guy's *goomar* will know another guy's *goomar*. Sometimes the girlfriends hang out. Sometimes the girlfriends introduce each other to guys—that's often how the goomba meets his *goomar,* because she's friends with someone else's *goomar.*

The other thing that makes it exciting is that every evening with the *goomar* is like a first date. You don't stay home with the *goomar.* You don't hang around the apartment. You go out. Your time together is limited, so it feels precious. When you get together, you're going to a show, or a restaurant, or a hotel, or you're sneaking out of town. It's not going to be just another humdrum night at home. It's going to be special.

Here are some rules for having a girlfriend.

GOOMAR GUIDELINES

DO: Take her to the movies.
DON'T: Take her to a peep show.

DO: Ask her out for a candlelight dinner.
DON'T: Ask her to help torch a restaurant for the insurance money.

DO: Take her to an amusement park.
DON'T: Take her to a trailer park.

If you don't keep the *goomar* relationship exciting, it gets boring. And if it gets boring, look out—because then, it's just like being married. One person or the other, the goomba or the *goomar,* is going to think, "If I needed this kind of aggravation, I'd get married." The goomba is going to think, "I get enough of this crap at home already." The *goomada* is going to think, "If I'm going to stay home every night, I want a prenup."

I've been married a long time. It's my first marriage. It's not a starter marriage. It's the real thing. I'm not going anywhere. Not that I think there's anything bad about people getting divorced and having second marriages and stepchildren and shared custody and all that stuff. I don't think it's *wrong*. I just think that it's like a heart attack: I'm sorry it happened to you, and I'm glad it didn't happen to me.

Keeping a marriage happy isn't all that complicated. You just gotta jump in with both feet, and stay in, the same way you do everything else. If you're taking your *goomada* to Atlantic City for the weekend, you better be taking your wife to Vegas. If you're going out to a nice dinner with all your pals on Friday night, you better have something special planned with the family for Saturday night. If you're buying yourself a beautiful new gold wristwatch that goes with the beautiful new gold chain that goes with the beautiful new sweat suit you bought yourself last week, you better ask the jeweler what he's got in a ladies timepiece, too.

It gets easier if you remember that most goomba marriages last longer than most goomba prison sentences. You're in for a long stretch. Better make the most of it.

Not all goombas think that way. They're old-fashioned. They think a woman's place is in the home, over the stove, where she's supposed to mind her own business and keep her mouth shut. You want a wife like that, I hope you get one. You're both going to be miserable. That's the goomba who comes home every night and starts yelling at his future ex-wife.

Here are some tips for a successful and long-lasting marriage:

GOOMBA HINTS FOR A HAPPY MARRIAGE

- There is no piece of clothing ever made that makes your wife look fat. No matter how many times she asks, the answer is, "No. You look good in that dress."
- Always tell your wife that you like her sauce better than your mother's. You can always make excuses to your mother if she hears about it.
- Never raise your hand to your wife, or your voice. The loudmouth guy who smacks his wife around is going to wind up like Joey Buttafuoco—a goomba who shoulda kept his mouth and his zipper shut.
- Always maintain good, open communication in your house—even if that means your wife throws plates while you try to explain where you've been.
- Never go to bed angry. Make sure one of you is drunk enough to just pass out without remembering that you were fighting.
- Always remember your wife's birthday, and your wedding anniversary. How hard could this be? Most goombas can remember every item on the menu at their favorite restaurant and all the batting averages for every player on the 1961 Yankees. This ain't world history. It's just two dates. And consider the penalty if you forget.
- Never be cheap with gifts. Give your wife an expensive piece of jewelry for her birthday—even if it means you have to actually *buy* it.

CHAPTER 6

Living *La Vida Goomba*

A lot of nice stuff has happened to me from being on *The Sopranos*. I got to move back to New York. I recently bought my own place. Wherever I go, a lot of people recognize me. I get invited to do all kinds of things that I used to dream about doing. I was invited to work out with the New York Knicks—me, an overweight, middle-aged guy who used to play basketball as a kid, and I got invited to work out with the New York Knicks! Like I'd died and gone to basketball heaven.

Another time, a bunch of us from the show went to Yankee Stadium, where we met the team and threw out the first pitch. George Steinbrenner gave us his box. My wife and kids flew in from Las Vegas, and I got to invite a few friends. There were 45,000 people there, on a Saturday afternoon. I walked out to the pitcher's mound and I thought, "I am never going to do this again."

That kind of thing doesn't happen every day, but it happens a

A great day in any goomba's life—throwing out the first pitch at Yankee Stadium.

lot. We get treated pretty special. We sit in the special seats. You think, "This is pretty cool."

If my daughter wants to see a kids' movie like *The Sisterhood of the Traveling Pants,* we go to the premiere. If my wife wants to see a new HBO production like *Empire Falls,* we go to the premiere. If I want to see Sting, I go to Atlantic City. A hotel there invited me. They sent a limo. My wife and I went, with one of our daughters. We got a suite in the hotel, and a big dinner, and then second-row seats to see Sting. We got back into the limo the next day and came home.

This is the Goomba Diet—living large and loving it.

But here's the thing. I *always* lived like that. Even when I had nothing, I knew how to enjoy what I had. I learned how to do that at a very young age.

Last summer I rented my family a huge house right on the water near Laguna Beach, California. We stayed a whole month. It's the first time we ever did that, even though we've been going to Laguna and Newport Beach for twenty years. For a long time we would go down for a week and stay in a fancy hotel. Before that, we would go down for a week and stay in a not-so-fancy hotel. Before that, we'd go down and stay in a pretty bad hotel. I remember paying $40 a night, and $100 a night, and then $400 a night.

I thought we were on top of the world when we stayed at the fancy hotel. I'd reserve a suite, and then when I got there I'd tip the concierge and make sure we were on the club level. It's like a special floor. The suites are the same, but there's a room on the level that's off-limits to the other guests. It has a TV and an open bar, and you get your breakfast and lunch there. Breakfast is coffee, Danishes, cereal, and juice. Lunch is finger sandwiches, a few pieces of fruit, beer, wine, full bar. Before dinner you would go there for mozzarella and tomato, peppers, cold cuts, a couple of martinis. Then you'd go out to dinner, and come back for a cognac. Everything but the dinner is free!

But before I could afford any of that, we'd still go to Laguna or Newport. We'd stay at the Comfort Inn or the Rodeway Inn. We'd leave Las Vegas early on a Friday morning, driving my '83 Camaro—my first new car ever. We'd drive down and we'd hit all the touristy spots, with names like Woody's and Rusty's. We'd spend the weekend on the beach. We'd go to Anaheim for an Angels game, or San Diego for a Padres game, or we'd go to Disneyland—even before we had kids.

No matter where we were staying, it was the same vacation. Today, my wife and I still go to the same beach we went to when we stayed at the Comfort Inn.

Even when we couldn't leave town, we'd try to make the weekend special. When my first daughter was really young, we'd go on vacation for the weekend without going out of town. I'd book one of the big suites at the Riviera—one of the big rooms with the sunken bathtub and the grand piano. I'd order a limo to pick us up. We'd check into the hotel and act like big shots. We'd order room service. We'd order movies and watch them in the room. We'd spend the whole weekend there.

That's a very goomba thing. If you're going, you go all the way.

Of course, not everybody is a goomba. Check this list and see.

YOU MIGHT BE A GOOMBA IF . . .

- You ask the car salesman about head room and leg room—in the trunk.
- You used to beat up other kids and leave their teeth under your pillow for the tooth fairy.
- The words "*gabagool*," "*pasta fazool*," and "*soopersat*" are part of your everyday vocabulary.

That might be a little confusing. If you got no idea what any of that means, you're probably not a goomba. If you're still not sure, here's another list:

YOU ARE NOT A GOOMBA IF . . .

- You wear bicycle pants.
- You've ever had a facial.
- Your pinkie ring has a whistle on it.
- Your favorite Martin Scorsese film is *The Age of Innocence.*

It's the same with food and drink. The goomba's going to have what he likes. I've been drinking the same Pinot Grigio forever. I don't care if I'm in a place that's got $400 bottles of wine, and someone else is paying. I drink what I drink. If I feel like lobster, I'm going to order the lobster. If I'm going out to dinner, I'm going out all the way.

I know people who don't live this way. They say, "What do you need an expensive hotel for? Why do you have to go to an expensive restaurant?"

I don't have to. I want to. I like to live good.

It wasn't like that when I was a kid. Growing up in the old neighborhood, we didn't have a lot of money to throw around.

I lived at the corner of Benson and Bay 11th Street in a two-story brick house. All the action was down the block at the corner

It's not Trump Towers, but you make do.

of Bath Avenue and 16th Street. There was a drugstore on one corner and a butcher on the other corner. Across the street was the
market my grandmother used to cook for. Over there was the pork
store. Down the street, Marino's Bakery had a ten-cent slice of
pizza. Frankie Pons was a luncheonette—a big bookie joint. The
Magic Lantern was a mob bar, and it had a bocce court behind it.
Over there was a toy store, where the old guy who ran it wouldn't
sell you a tube of glue unless you were buying a model car or
model airplane. So naturally all the glue sniffers would go in and
buy a model airplane and a tube of glue. Outside the store, they'd
throw the model on the sidewalk and go sniff the glue. That's
where my friends and I got our model airplanes and cars—off the
sidewalk. We couldn't afford to buy our own.

My friends would meet at the drugstore every night and hang out—maybe twenty or thirty of us. We didn't have much of anything between us.

My family was the poorest family I knew. Most of the other kids had mothers and fathers. The fathers worked, and the mothers stayed home. I had a father, but he was away from the house a lot, and he wasn't contributing much. So my mother worked all the time. How she kept the family together I don't know. Partly because she wouldn't take no for an answer, and she made sure we were taken care of. If I didn't have money to play ball, if there was a uniform to pay for or sign-up money to pay, she'd write a note. Somebody paid—I don't know who. It wasn't her, and it wasn't my father, but she always found a way. She'd write a letter to the guy who owned the shoe store on Bath Avenue. She'd write a letter to the guy who ran the store where you'd buy your school uniform— the white shirt and the school pants and the little red assembly tie. I'd go in with a note saying she was going to pay at the end of the month but I needed something now. The stores would honor those notes. Sometimes my sneakers had holes in them, and I remember having to stick cardboard in the shoes to keep my socks from coming out, but I always had shoes.

Same with food. You'd go in with a shopping list and a note saying that you couldn't pay until Friday, and they'd run you a tab. Or you'd go in with a check on Friday and say, "Please, don't take this to the bank until next week."

But even then, when you had nothing, you tried to be generous. My mother had a rule: Never walk in empty-handed. If you're going to a party or visiting a sick friend or going to someone's house for dinner, you always bring a little something. "I don't care what's in your hands," she said. "But you don't go in with nothing."

On a Sunday afternoon, I'd say, "Can I go have dinner with Bobby?" And she'd say, "Okay. But take something." I'd get an Italian bread, or a pastry, or a box of doughnuts or a pound of cookies.

Even my father used to tell me to be generous. When I was leaving the house, he would say, "Do you have any money?" Of course I didn't have any money! I never had any money. He would give me a dollar and say, "Never leave the house with no money."

He was a rotten father in a lot of ways. He was a gambler, and he didn't support his family. He would whine about a horse coming in second—for a week! The next twenty people he met, he would say, "I can't catch a fuckin' break!"

As a family, we never had any steady money. I remember as a kid, when we were broke, telling my father, "Maybe if you didn't play the horses . . ."

He screamed at me, "Don't tell me what to do with my money!"

But when he hit, it was like Christmas. He was very generous when he won. If he had money, he gave it up. Everybody got something.

Unlike me and my friends, there were guys in the neighborhood who seemed to have money all the time. You didn't know what they did to get the money, and you didn't ask, but you saw them and you wondered.

When we were teenagers and we started going out and about, we'd see these guys at the clubs. You'd see them driving up in their Cadillacs and Lincolns. They had chrome rims, and they were waxed, and maybe they had pin-striping. The guys driving them looked perfect. They had expensive suits, and nice leather coats in the winter. They wore these expensive Giorgio Brutini shoes. You could see the big pinky ring. You'd hear about them getting the manicure, getting their nails buffed. They'd have the gold chain and the cross, or the gold chain and the horn—to ward off the evil eye.

Some of these guys who looked like a million bucks might have actually been broke. They might have stolen or borrowed everything they had. It didn't matter, as long as they looked good.

We tried to do the same thing when we got older. My friend Bo's father was a longshoreman and he used to buy a brand-new Cadillac every two years—a Cadillac convertible Eldorado. So Bo would borrow the car and we'd go driving around the neighborhood. We had no money, not even for gas. Bo would have to drive by his house and steal money out of his mother's purse, just so we could keep driving.

We called that kind of car a Dad-illac. Or Daddy's Caddy.

It wasn't just us. Lots of guys we knew were scrounging for money. There was a tradition back then that, when a guy bought a new car, he'd drive through the neighborhood real slow. He'd pull up to the curb and all his friends would throw a buck, or five bucks, or fifty cents into the car. I knew one guy who spent every dime he had on his new ride, and then drove it around the neighborhood just for gas money.

Not all the guys I knew were broke. Some of them were older than us. We'd see them on a Saturday or Sunday, when we were playing ball, and we'd listen to them talk about going out. I was sixteen. I would hear them talking about going to this club or that club. I remember one time a guy said he spent $68 last night. I couldn't even imagine that. It was a fortune!

Most of these guys had been very poor when they were young. I remember one guy named Richie. His family was Italian, from Bari—the Barese, they called themselves. When he was a little boy, the Barese did all the ice delivery in New York in the summer, and all the coal in the winter. Richie grew up delivering from the age of ten. He'd go with his father on a horse-drawn wagon. Because he was young and strong, they'd pull up in front of a building and tell him apartment A or apartment B. They never had to say which floor. If they were sending Richie, by himself, it was always the top floor.

He was poor. He got a dollar a day. He lived in a walk-up apartment with no hot water. He'd take a bath, once a week, at the public baths. It cost him ten cents.

So, later, when he had some money, Richie knew how to enjoy himself. He knew how to dress, and eat, and take care of people. Because he had seen the other side of it. That made him tough, and it made him appreciate the good things.

For other guys it was all about image. I knew a guy who mixed his own cologne. He'd mix up some Lagerfeld, and Givenchy, and Pierre Cardin, his own formula. He'd say, "I don't want to go out at night smelling like everybody else." After you shook his hand, you'd remember the smell.

We weren't living large in my family. A big day out for us was Coney Island. My mother would pack up a cooler full of tuna fish sandwiches and lemonade and we'd take the bus down to the beach. We'd spend the whole day there, playing in the water, hanging out, having a ball. And at night there were fireworks. We'd stay until the end, then take the bus back home. It was great.

But I knew there was something else. By the time I was in college, I was always dead broke. I'd take the train into Manhattan and walk around. I'd see these guys in expensive suits, going into these big restaurants, the steak houses, and I'd think, "How do you make that happen?"

My father, before that, was a bartender at Shea Stadium for a while. He'd take me to work with him sometimes, and I'd watch him serving drinks in the Diamond Club, which is the private room at the stadium for VIPs. There were guys in nice golf shirts and pants. My father would be serving them their drinks, and I would think, "Okay, how do you get there? How do you get that?" I would stare at the guys sitting in the good seats, and think, "Who are they? How come they get to sit down there?"

Well, now I know. Now *I'm* doing it. Now I sit at center court for the Knicks games. And I get a huge kick out of it. I remember breaking my ass to get $12 together to take my girl to see a Knicks game when I was in college. We sat up in the highest tip-top cheap seats. Now I take my daughters to the game, and we sit right down in the action. We go an hour before the game, sometimes, and eat in the private dining room.

Some people would say, "What's the big deal?" To me, it's a big deal. I get a thrill out of it. I've gotten to meet a lot of nice people—celebrities, newscasters, sports figures—people I'd never meet otherwise. Me, a kid from Bay 11th Street.

Almost the first job I ever had, as a kid, was with the park department in Brooklyn when I was in college. I was supposed to be working at some basketball courts. And I was—working out, that is. I'd show up and play basketball, all day long, and for that I drew a paycheck. It was all arranged, the way those things are arranged. Some guys go through their whole lives working jobs like that—jobs arranged by the unions, or a friend in the unions, or a friend on the docks, or whatever.

That was the last easy job I ever had. Since then, I've been working pretty hard. I never minded that. I like working hard. Most goombas do. They're blue-collar guys, for the most part. They expect to get up early and go to a job, and work hard for their money, and come home at the end of the day having done a good day's work.

That's part of the Goomba Diet, too. Your working man does his job the same way he does everything else. If he's in, he's all the way in. He ain't loafing. He might've gone into his father's business, but he's trying hard to make it bigger.

That's the way they live because it's the way they have to live. They want the good things in life. They want to provide for their families. So how are they gonna do that without working hard? If you're not gonna be a thief, where's that money coming from?

That's why most goombas really hustle. Michael Imperioli's dad was a New York bus driver, with a route in the Bronx. Michael remembers his father working hard, ridiculously long shifts, and then adding two hours to his day when he moved his family upstate for a better life when Michael was in high school. He drove that bus for thirty years.

Michael said, "That instilled in me a sense that, no matter what you do, you better work *hard*. You better treat it with respect."

Not all goombas live that way, of course. My own father was a
good example of how *not* to work. He had an injury when he was
in his late thirties and he never worked an honest day in his life
after that. He was on disability. He had a scam going here and a
scam going there. He lay on the couch for thirty years, doing nothing but complaining.

Some guys make a career of scamming. You'll see men around
the neighborhood who don't work. They've always got a little
thing going—an insurance scam, a disability scam, something
under the table, something not quite legal. They make a big score,
and start getting $800 a month disability. Like that's some kind of
deal! But they'll work for months trying to set up something like
that for themselves. Or they'll have some little job they do on the
side, off the books—working as a waiter, or a cook, or a driver or
a delivery man. They'll use someone else's Social Security number
so they're not on the radar.

On the other hand, you walk around the neighborhood and you
see these retired guys sitting on the stoop in the evening. They go
to the park and play bocce during the daytime. They sit in the café
and drink espresso. They go home for lunch. It's a simple life.
These guys might have worked a lot of years on the docks, or delivering mail, or whatever. Now, they're taking it easy. They're not
exactly banging around town all night long. This is all they do. It's
simple, and they like it that way. They're content to sit on the stoop
and watch the world go by.

That could've been me. Any of these guys could've been me,
including the wise guys. I look at all the kids I grew up with. Some
of them went left and some of them went right. I got no idea why.
When I walk through the neighborhood now and say hello to the
people I meet, half the guys on the street just got out of jail. You
see them sitting on the stoop, or standing on the corner, and it's
like they never left the block. Then you bump into somebody else,
and he says, "So you saw Paulie, right? He just got out of the joint.
Five years for armed robbery. . . . It's his third stretch."

Who knows why? What makes the difference? We all came from the same place. We all had the same influences. Who knows what makes one guy go this way and the other guy go the other way?

There were gangsters in the neighborhood when I was a kid. They were rich and powerful and everyone knew who they were. If someone was in trouble, they'd show up and spread a little money around. If someone needed a job, they'd put in a good word. If you're a kid and your dad is a plumber or a mailman, that kind of wise guy can be pretty impressive. If you're a kid and you don't have a dad, or your dad is a bum, or he's out of work and he's been out of work forever, that guy is *very* impressive. Some people I know were drawn to that life and never looked back.

There's good jobs for the goomba and there's bad jobs for the goomba. He could be the cop, or he could be the robber. He could make a good Pope, or a good mayor of New York City, but he probably wouldn't make a good Supreme Court Justice, or a good Imam or Ayatollah. Not that he couldn't do it, but the goomba probably isn't going to be happy working as a florist. It's just not his style. Here are some guidelines.

GOOD GOOMBA JOBS
- Bouncer.
- Bail bondsman.
- "Muscle."
- Lounge singer.

BAD GOOMBA JOBS
- Ambassador.
- Professional ice skater.
- Hog caller.
- Imperial Wizard.

It's nothing to be ashamed of. It's just the truth. You almost never hear a goomba addressed as "Senator" or "Dean." The only time a goomba is going to hear the words "Your Honor" is when he's about to enter a plea.

A goomba could be a sex maniac, but he's probably not going to be a gynecologist. He might love to travel, but you almost never read about goomba flight attendants. He might love music, but you will never see a goomba hip-hop artist or mariachi singer. You won't meet a goomba yodeler. Even if you could run ads in the papers and hire a private investigator, you still could not find a goomba female impersonator—except Frank Marino, who's a goomba from Brooklyn who appears in

Who says there's no goomba drag queens? Brooklyn's own Frank Marino.

"Evening at La Cage" in Vegas. That must be the exception that proves the rule.

There are some jobs you wouldn't automatically think are good for goombas, but I know some goombas who do them well. Hairdresser, for example, is out. But barber is in. My friend Silvio has a barbershop in Bay Ridge. He's been cutting hair there so long that he was cutting *my* hair when I was a teenager. He's a great barber and a good guy. His whole family is barbers. His brother invented Tony Sirico's wings—the silver stripes in Paulie Walnuts's hair. Silvio's brothers immigrated from Calabria in 1967 and opened the store. Silvio came a couple of years later. He still charges only $10 for a haircut, and he takes his work seriously.

I also know a lot of goombas who could be called entrepreneurs. They're in business for themselves—don't ask what business, exactly—and they're smart and clever and successful.

Silvio (far right) and the boys, still cutting hair in Bay Ridge.

I had one friend who was arrested on suspicion of doing something illegal, like, say, bookmaking. The cops arrested him at his new home, a million-dollar house that he had just moved into. He was unemployed, officially, and had no visible means of support. So the cops were surprised when they found $200,000 in cash hidden in the ceiling.

He didn't offer an explanation. "Who knows?" he said. "Maybe it came with the house."

You gotta love a guy like that.

My first job in Las Vegas was delivering pizza. I had a 1969 Javelin. I would work from six in the evening until midnight. I was paid $20, plus tips, for the shift. It was all off the books, so I did all right. You'd earn a few bucks from tips, plus I had an arrangement with the guy who made the pizzas. Every night, we'd take some orders and he'd make a few pizzas that were off the books. I'd go south with a couple pizzas and collect the money for pizzas that, technically, were never ordered. He and I would split the money.

The $20 went into a drawer when I got home. That money was for expenses. I was splitting the rent with three other guys, including my friends Puddy and Bo from back home. The rent was $700 a month, and we had to pay for gas and electricity and the telephone and all that. The rest of the pizza money was going-out money.

Over the years I had all kinds of jobs. I was a chimney sweep. I worked in a fruit store. I worked on a soda truck for a guy who had the 7-Up route. I was also, for a very short time, a bartender. I hated it. It's bad enough you gotta work around people for a living, but here you're trapped. You gotta stand there listening to all this crap, and act like you're interested. They're tipping you, so they think they own a piece of you. It was terrible, and I didn't last too long. Then I started working as a bouncer. After that, I got a job as the entertainment director at the Riviera Hotel.

Whatever I did, I did it all the way. I jumped in feet first. When I was a bouncer, I wanted to find out everything about being a bouncer—who the other bouncers in town were, how they handled stuff, how they got paid, all that.

I found out there's a lot more to being a bouncer than punching some guy in the face. I found out that you never grab a guy in the club and say, "Get out." You always tap him on the shoulder and say, "Could I speak to you outside for a minute?" That way, if there's a problem, it happens outside. I found out that the last thing you want to do is fight. I found out that, if you have to fight, you make sure the other guy throws the first punch—so, if there's a lawsuit, you can say you were protecting yourself. If he files charges, *you* file charges. I found out that you can't tolerate a drunk who's loud and obnoxious. A guy told me, "If a guy is drunk and acting up when he comes in, remember: He's not going to get any better after he has a couple of drinks in him."

I learned that bouncers had little side businesses. One of them was making sure the pimps and hookers were paying for the privilege of using the club as their workplace. When they left, they'd have to pay. I'd shake hands with a pimp, and say, "When we break, there'd better be a twenty in there for me or you're not coming back." If a hooker was leaving with a guy, she'd have to pay me five or ten bucks. That's the way the business works.

I treated being a bouncer as a serious, full-time job. And it was. I was making $40,000 a year, in cash, in 1982. That wasn't bad.

When I was a maître d' I had no idea what that was all about. The Riviera had an empty room with some tables and chairs. They said, "Make a showroom." So I took all that information I got as a bouncer and expanded it. I learned more.

When I got the job booking comedy acts at the Improv, I learned about that, too. I didn't know anything when I started. Budd Friedman? Never heard of him. I knew nothing about comedy. But I jumped in and I learned. I visited comedy clubs. I went to Improvs in other cities. I talked to the guys who knew. I found out who was good to work with and who wasn't, and how much money the comics made, and how you paid them, and how much time they got on stage, and how to get them off stage. I learned how to handle the rough stuff. It seems simple now, but I didn't know that you don't grab a heckler when he's heckling. You wait. You don't try to shut him up when a comic's on stage. You tap him on the shoulder and ask him if you can speak to him for a minute—after the guy goes off. Otherwise, you make it worse.

I learned who all the good comics were, and which ones were a pain in the ass. I got to be friends with Denis Leary, Damon Wayans, George Lopez, and Rosie O'Donnell, a lot of people who are still my friends today.

I learned who some of the problem guys were, too. There was one guy who had a very successful career as an impressionist, in the 1970s. But now he was a falling-down drunk. He had moved to Las Vegas and was trying to pull himself together. He used to come to the club and watch the younger comics. I told Budd Friedman, "Let's give the guy a shot."

He packed it in, the night he opened. I had people literally stuffing my pockets with money to get a good seat. I finally had to leave the floor, to empty my pockets because money was falling out of them.

Backstage, the impressionist has his pants down around his ankles. He's got his cock and his balls out, and he's dipping them into a bucket of ice water. I said, "Put that away! You're supposed to be on!"

Maybe this was his way of staying sober. But between sets, he went down to the casino and got bombed. I had to take him off before he finished his second set.

My mistake. Everybody makes them. A friend of mine was entertainment director at a hotel. They asked him to book a New Year's act. They wanted Robert Goulet and Debbie Reynolds. Well, they weren't available. My friend said, "What about Sam Butera?" He was Louis Prima's sax player. He's a great guy and a great performer, and he has a terrific act. They said, "Great! You can get a Louis Prima impersonator and a Keely Smith impersonator to work with him!" My friend said, "That's insulting. I won't even ask." Can you imagine? He played with the real thing. It would be like asking Art Garfunkel to perform with a Paul Simon impersonator.

Even today, though, you see a lot of that. They had a show at one of the hotels called The Concert That Never Was—Sinatra and Streisand. There's a Billy Idol impersonator in Vegas. And a Willie Nelson impersonator. Not for nothing, but I don't even want to see the *real* Billy Idol. Look at all these Rat Pack shows. Do people really want to see a Joey Bishop impersonator?

Like a comedian I know said, "What's next, a Frank Sinatra *Jr.* impersonator?"

Who knows? Maybe being the Frank Sinatra Jr. impersonator is a good job. For most goombas, it wouldn't be. For a little more guidance on which gigs are good and which ones aren't, here's another list:

BAD GOOMBA OCCUPATIONS

- Lighthouse keeper.
- Ski instructor.
- Pool boy.
- Rabbi.
- Simultaneous translator.

It's not that the goomba is stupid. Far from it. You try running a numbers racket, and keeping all that stuff in your head. He's gotta be a genius. But he's not going to be a rocket scientist. He might be good with his hands, but he's not going to be a massage therapist. He could be very good at making things disappear, but he's not going to be a magician. He knows all about morning wood, but he ain't no lumberjack.

When I started acting, I took it seriously. The first job I got was a little comic bit, on film, for a Fox TV show called *Sunday Night Comics.* I played a mob guy who was robbing people on golf courses. A friend asked me to do the bit, so I flew down to Los Angeles, on my own time and with my own money.

I got a huge charge out of doing it. On the way home, I was sky high. Then it aired, and I got calls from all kinds of people. I couldn't wait to do it again.

So I did it again: I got another acting job as soon as I could. I did a bit on *America's Funniest People.* Then I did a thing on *Up All Night* with Rhonda Shear. Then Drew Carey put me in something he was doing. Kevin Pollak put me in his HBO special. Then I met a casting director, Ray Favero, when I got this little part in Martin Scorsese's *Casino,* and Ray started helping me think about acting. I bought books on acting and studied Michael Caine's tapes on acting. Later, after I got the job on *The Sopranos,* I got an acting coach, Richard Scanlon, who I still work with today.

In other words, I always treated acting like a job. I didn't think, "This is it. I've arrived." I was always trying to get better and better.

Even now, I don't get every job I go up for. Sometimes I get an audition and I read and I prepare and I go in and it just doesn't happen. I know I'm not the best actor in the world, and I know I'm not the best guy for every role. But when I get called in to read for someone, I do the very best I can. I may not be the guy, but I give it a shot.

One time, I read for something opposite Chuck Norris. I did a great job. But think about it. He's about 5-foot-8. I'm about 6 feet. He's the star of the show. There's no way I'm going to get that part.

But I gave it a shot.

When I started writing books, I was the same way. I never read a book review in my life until it was part of my job. Whose book is coming out? Who cares? I had no interest in that. Now I read the *New York Times Book Review* every week. I've asked a million questions and learned all about the book business. I learn what's successful and what's not. That's why, when we do a book signing, we make it a whole event. Some guys just show up and sign books. We show up with Italian music on a boom box and a tray of meatballs. When we do a signing, it's a party. Sometimes the people at the signing *make* it a party. I've had people come to my book signings armed with wine, cheese, and sausages. Remember my mother said, "Don't show up empty-handed?" These people were showing respect by bringing a little something to say thank you.

I show my respect by coming to the job site ready to do the work. It's all about commitment. When I go on the Conan O'Brien show, I'm prepared. Some actors seem to think all they have to do is show up and answer questions. Not me. I've studied. I've watched the show. I see what works and what doesn't. I see the guests who go on and they're horrible. They might be intelligent and charming. They might be big stars. But they got nothing to say. People at home are saying, "Wow. She's beautiful. And she's stupid."

That's not for me. I look at it like a performance. From the beginning, I thought of it as another part of my job. My first talk show was Craig Kilborn. Now I'm doing my fifteenth or sixteenth appearance on *The Tonight Show*—about half of those as a regular correspondent. I look at it this way: There's six million people sitting at home watching this. They're expecting to be entertained. I have to entertain them.

The last thing I want is for people at home to be asking themselves, "Who does that fat bastard think he is?" That would kill me.

So I work at it. I prepare material. I practice lines. I put together a little monologue. I rehearse it. By the time I get to the show, I'm ready.

It's the goomba way. The other day I bumped into Tony Sirico, who plays Paulie Walnuts on the show. He had just gotten a new script. I said, "How's it going with the new pages?" He said, "I eat that script. I eat that script for lunch and dinner. I devour that script."

That's the goomba at work. That's the way Tony started his working life—when he was a kid. Tony's first job was plucking chickens, for a quarter a chicken. He was eleven. He delivered papers at fourteen. He had a job as a roofer. He worked on high-rises, as an ironworker, walking those beams above the thirty-sixth floor. He treated each of those jobs like it was the only job he'd ever have, and he was going to do it right.

I feel like I gotta do it the same way. Otherwise, you watch. In ten years, I'll be on an episode of *The Surreal Life,* with Danny Bonaduce and one of the Olsen twins.

While I was working all these jobs in Vegas, and learning the ropes, I was also learning how to live the Goomba Diet way—even though I had no idea that's what it was. I was learning how to live life to the fullest.

In the old days, back when I was delivering pizzas, I got off at midnight. That was perfect for Las Vegas because nobody went out until two o'clock anyway. Me and my friends would go out and meet people. I got to know a lot of gamblers. I learned how they lived.

The whole city ran on tips. Money didn't just talk. It danced and screamed. If you tipped big, you could live like royalty, whether you were a cabdriver or the president of the hotel. Taking care of people got you respect. I saw regular people get treated great. They got respect. They got broads! They'd go into a place like the Palace Court restaurant, at Caesars Palace, and be treated like kings.

My friend Mikey Dell was out in Vegas before I was. He showed me the ropes. He taught me how to behave. He said, "Always tip. Always dress nice. Always, before you go into a place, give the maître d' twenty bucks."

I learned. I did what I was told. It worked! After I entered the business and became a bouncer, I got to know a lot of people. Sometimes, instead of a tip, people would "comp" me someplace, or they'd give me tickets to something. I started going to all the big fights. There was one regular customer who was a big poker player. He'd win, playing poker . . . then lose everything playing blackjack and baccarat. But he'd give me tickets to anything I wanted at Caesars Palace. I learned how the system worked.

So, when my mother came to visit, for the first time, we sat in the third row to see Sinatra. I'd been given the tickets, and when we got there I gave the maître d' twenty bucks, and I gave the waiter twenty bucks. We got the best seats, and I never saw a check. It was all comped.

I saw every show in town that way. I saw Diana Ross. I saw the Beach Boys and Sammy Davis Jr. I saw Liberace. I went everywhere, and I was always comped, and I always got the best seats—because I took care of the maître d' and I took care of the waiter. The poker player would tell the maître d' to take care of me. I'd go in and order dinner and bottles of Dom Perignon. I made sure I tipped good, and this guy was such a big gambler that no one ever questioned it. I never saw a check. I went to Michael's, at the Barbary Coast, which was a very exclusive restaurant at that time. It, too, was all comped.

And I couldn't believe it. I'm thinking, "I'm from Brooklyn. I'm twenty-two. I'm in the third row at Caesars, watching Frank Sinatra! How did that happen?"

Over time I learned how to behave. I remember one time, when I was first working as a bouncer, a heavy guy came in and said to me, "Watch my back, will ya?" Then he gave me a hundred-dollar bill. I was stunned! I called a friend of mine from the pay phone and said, "You won't believe this. Some guy just gave me a hundred-dollar tip!"

Awhile back me and some of *The Sopranos* guys were doing this appearance in Lake Tahoe. Vince Curatola, Johnny "Sack" on the show, is a great singer, and sometimes he likes to sing in lounges. Well, we were in a lounge, and there was a piano player. I went up to him and asked if he'd mind playing along so my friend could sing. I tipped him a hundred bucks. I gotta admit, it felt good to do that.

Not that just throwing money around is going to do you any good. If you're not enjoying it, why bother? I've seen lots of compulsive guys over the years who threw their money away on nothing, and had nothing to show for it when it was over.

I knew guys when I lived in Vegas who would get paid on a Friday afternoon, before working their shift from six o'clock in the evening until two o'clock in the morning, then going home. Instead, they'd pick up the check right before work, at five forty-five. At seven they'd go on a break. They'd cash their check, run across the street to another casino, and by seven fifteen they'd be broke. They'd lose the whole thing, a week's wages, by the end of their first break. Then they'd come back to the hotel and finish the shift.

I used to know construction workers in Vegas who were making pretty good money. They would bring their paychecks to these local bars, where you would get two free drinks if you cashed your paycheck there. These guys would work from six in the morning until two in the afternoon, in the summer. They'd come in at two thirty, cash that check, and never leave. By the time it was five in

Vince and Jim out on the town, and no, it's not a scene from the show.

the morning again, they'd be broke, and drunk, and have to go back to work. Brutal.

I knew extreme gamblers, sick gamblers, who would bet on the horses all day long and then bet on basketball and football at night. I knew guys who went broke, who stole from their families, who wrote bad checks, who went to jail. . . . There was no end to how far down they could go.

Is that you? There are warning signs that you might have a problem.

YOU MIGHT BE A PROBLEM GAMBLER IF . . .

- You put your kid on the merry-go-round and lay a bet on his horse.
- You pay your kids' allowance in casino chips. Or markers.
- When you were a kid, you always doubled-down on Go Fish.
- You've ever played Russian roulette and bet against yourself.

That's not what I'm talking about. I'm talking about having a good time.

But you gotta do it right.

When I was in college, I was poor all the time. My friends were always paying for stuff for me—dinner, drinks, tickets to something. Later on, when I had money, I tried to return the favor. My friends would come out to Las Vegas and nothing was too good for them. I'd get them tickets to all the shows, make sure their meals were all comped, make sure they got treated right in the casino. I wasn't showing off. I was just trying to pay back a little of what they'd given me.

When I visited New York, I'd try to take them out there, too. We'd go out to a fancy place for dinner, and I'd blow a bunch of money on a big dinner and a couple of nice bottles of wine.

When I'd get home, my father would look up from the couch and say, "Where'd you go?" I'd tell him. He'd say, "Expensive. Who paid?" I'd tell him. "How much was it?" I'd tell him.

Then he'd start yelling, "How dare you throw your money around like that? Don't you realize how much I could use that kind of money? You should spend that money on your family!"

I was already giving my mother money every month. As for my father, I told him, "Maybe if you got your ass off that couch and tried to make a living, you wouldn't be so broke all the time."

I was already learning something he never learned—that if you work hard, you can play hard. That if you earned the money honest, you could go spend it honest, and have fun doing it. It's not like I stole the money and I don't know where the next heist is coming from. It's not like it fell into my lap and I got no idea where to get any more of it. I worked for it. I earned it. I got a job. If I lose the job, I can get another job. So what I do with the money is my business, and what I want to do with it is have fun.

I had also learned from being in Las Vegas that there was a right way and a wrong way to throw your money around. I had already seen the loudmouth goomba come in. He hits the casino with a fat bankroll and starts waving it around at the tables, peeling off a twenty here and a fifty there, ordering people around. He grabs the waitress and says, "Here's twenty bucks. Keep them drinks coming." He grabs the waiter and says, "Here's twenty bucks. Go get me some sandwiches." When he craps out at the craps table, he tosses a fifty-dollar chip at the dealer and says, "Get better dice." This isn't a guy who's telling people what he needs and offering to pay for it. This is a guy who's throwing his weight around. This ain't part of the Goomba Diet. This is part of the Asshole Diet. And nobody wants to be on that.

Instead, I try to remember what it was like for me when I was a working guy who depended on tips for my rent money. I try to remember that you should never embarrass anyone in public if you want them to give you good service. You should never treat them as less than you, just because you're buying and they're not.

So when I pull into the valet, I tuck a ten-dollar bill in my hand and I slide it to the guy when I give him the keys and say, "I'm going to be ten minutes. Keep the car up front, will ya?" When I get to the restaurant and I see it's crowded and people are waiting at the bar, I tuck a twenty-dollar bill in my hand and I go over and say hello to the maître d'. I pass him the twenty when I shake his hand. I don't point at a table and say, "We wanna sit there." I just shake his hand and say, "We're starving. See if you can squeeze us in."

I didn't have any training in this kind of finesse from my parents. When I was a kid, we didn't eat in restaurants or go to nightclubs. My mother loved Chinese food, and sometimes we would go out for Chinese. But that was unusual. Ninety-nine percent of the time we ate at home. I don't remember my father taking us out at all. So I didn't see goombas in action, up close, handling waiters and bartenders and maître d's.

My father would sometimes tell me how to behave. I remember him saying, before I went out on dates, "Don't forget to tip the maître d'. Don't forget to tip the hostess." Sometimes I remembered, and sometimes I didn't. Either way, I didn't really know what I was doing.

I was dating this one girl and she liked to go to this restaurant in Manhattan that had lots of little romantic tables. Almost every

My grandmother holding her favorite goomba, who started drinking young.

table was a quiet table in the corner. But the maître d' would always hustle everyone for at least one drink. He'd say, "I'm sorry, but I don't have anything right at this moment. You can wait at the bar." Then, as soon as you'd ordered and paid for your drink, the table was magically ready—the same table that had been sitting there, empty, the whole time. I never figured out that I could have just sat down at the table, right away, if I'd only slipped the guy five bucks.

One night, I took my girl to see Jackie Mason perform somewhere. The maître d' took us to the most horrible table in the whole place. We started to sit down. I was going to yell at the guy for giving us a crappy table. Then I remembered. I slipped the maître d' a five-dollar bill, and said, "Do you think we could get a little closer to the stage?" He said, "Certainly, sir," and took us right to the front row.

That was 1977. I was a junior goomba. I felt like I'd discovered a new continent or something. That's how new this stuff was to me. I had a lot to learn.

Tipping is not just a goomba thing, of course. But goombas are good at it. We've had practice. I've been watching guys do this since I was a kid. Guys who knew what they wanted were willing to pay a little extra for it. They weren't pushing anybody around. They weren't bribing anybody. They were just saying, "I'd like to be treated right, so I'm gonna start off by treating *you* right."

They were also announcing who they were. They were saying they wanted to be taken seriously. They were saying that they weren't tightwads, which in the goomba community is a bad thing to be.

If you get a reputation for being cheap, people talk about it. Around the neighborhood, we always knew who the cheap guys were. "He throws nickels around like they were manhole covers," they'd say. Or, "He took out a five-dollar bill and Lincoln was squinting," because it was so long since he'd seen the daylight.

You don't want people talking that way about you, right?

But there's right ways and wrong ways to do it. Years ago I heard a story about a wise guy who had made a big score and was celebrating with all his friends. They ate a huge dinner, drank gallons of wine, stayed in this place for hours, and had a lot of laughs. At the end of the evening, the wise guy called over the maître d' and said, "Lemme ask you something. What's the biggest tip you ever got?"

The maître d' said, "Five hundred dollars, sir."

The wise guy whipped out his bankroll and peeled off ten hundred-dollar bills. "There," he said. "Now it's a thousand!"

The maître d' was impressed. The guys were all impressed. But then the wise guy made a mistake. He pushed it a little too far. He called the maître d' back over to the table.

"Lemme ask you something else. The biggest tip you ever got before tonight—when did you get that? And who was it from?"

The maître d' cleared his throat and said, "It was about six months ago, sir. And it was from you."

You throw money around like that, you can't win.

Sometimes tipping is just plain logic. You always tip someone where you have the opportunity to pay up front for a little extra service—the valet parking guy, the car wash guy, and so on. You always tip someone who you know you're going to see again, and who you want the same good service from every time—the doorman at your apartment, the waiter at your favorite restaurant. You never tip someone who is doing a crappy job and you'll never see again, unless it's just the waiter and then he still gets his 15 percent. You also never tip someone who is already being paid just for doing what he's doing—like your business manager, your lawyer, or your bail bondsman.

It's a question of style. When I was young I'd sometimes see these wise guys or half-a-wiseguys throwing around money in the bars and clubs. They'd be buying everybody drinks, duking everybody a five, a ten, showing off. You always understood these guys had made some kind of score.

Later, I saw the cooler guys doing it right. They'd go into a crowded restaurant like Peter Luger's, and the maître d' would tell them it's going to be a while, and they'd say, "That's okay. Just do what you can." Pretty soon they've got a table, when a bunch of other people are still waiting at the bar. They shake the maître d's hand and give him the old palmer—a twenty, tucked in the palm, for taking care of them. The next time they come in, believe me, the maître d' is going to remember them. Like, probably better than he remembers who was first of all those people waiting at the bar.

Sometimes it's just practical. I have a friend who goes to the track a lot. Sometimes he wins. He hit a horse for $10,000 recently. The teller at the window was a friend of his. He reminded him that if he collected winnings of that amount, he'd have to pay tax on it. The track has to report it. But if he had someone else collect the winnings, he could duck the tax. Naturally the teller knew a guy—an old guy who hangs around the track and because of his age gets some tax break. My friend paid the guy $500 to collect his $10,000, and the IRS never knew what hit them.

Is that confusing? Here are some guidelines on who to duke and who not to duke:

GOOMBA TIPPING ETIQUETTE

* ALWAYS tip . . .
  . . . the bartender.
  . . . your barber.
  . . . the dealer.
  . . . the lap dancer.

* NEVER tip . . .
  . . . a policeman.
  . . . a congressman.
  . . . your clergyman.
  . . . your surgeon.

I worked for tips for a long time. I got tipped as a chimney sweep, when I was a teenager. And of course I worked for tips as a pizza delivery man. I got tipped as a bouncer, when I worked at Paul Anka's club, Jubilation, and at The Brewery. I got tipped as a maître d' at the Riviera Hotel and Casino. So I saw guys give 'em in all kinds of ways.

The weirdest tip I ever got was when I was working in Vegas at The Brewery. There were two sets of double doors, one leading to the street and one leading to the club. The bouncers usually waited in between the two doors. One night a guy came in and said, "My friends are outside. Will you throw me out of here?"

"Will I what?"

"I'll give you fifty bucks to throw me out of the club."

"Okay. Wait a second."

I got another bouncer. We grabbed this guy and rammed him head first through the doors. We threw him onto the street. I kicked him in the ass. I gave him a really professional throwing-out treatment.

Was he showing off for his friends? Winning a bet? I never found out.

Most of what I learned about tipping other people was more straightforward. It was all about getting the right kind of service.

When I lived in Vegas I knew some guys who, every once in a while, would ask me to come with them to make some "drops." They had people that took care of them. Here's a maître d'. Here's a bartender. Here's a doorman. Here's a dealer. So every once in a while, and always on a Sunday night, we'd go make some drops. We'd go to the bar at Caesars and leave the bartender a few extra bucks. We'd go to a restaurant and give the maître d' a few extra bucks. It was just our way of saying thank you, of giving a little back.

I learned how the city operated from real experts. When I first moved to Las Vegas, I lived in this apartment building where there were a lot of bookies. This was just coincidence, but it was good for me, because the pros taught me what I needed to know.

One of the first guys I met was Joe Rico. He was a bookie, and a hustler, and a real Vegas guy. He was short, and loud, and he'd come from Queens with nothing but a toothbrush and a wad of cash. He worked the sports book at the Stardust. This was in the days before the Internet, of course. So he'd go down to the Stardust, first thing, and start calling guys all over the country to tell them what was the line in the sports book—what were the odds on this game or that game. These guys would place bets with him.

Joe had terminal cancer. He was living on borrowed time. So he was all out—hookers, booze, pot, coke, whatever, he did it all. And he tipped everybody. He spread it around. In fact, he and a guy named Pete Cigars even had some doctors that they tipped. And some nurses. He'd tip the nurses to get an appointment, then tip the doctor to write a prescription. He'd fill the prescriptions, for Dilaudid, and then sell the pills to finance his other interests.

Every single night of the week, Joe Rico would take me and maybe six or seven other guys out to dinner. He took care of everything, and always with cash. He knew how to live, and he lived big. I watched him, one night, turn $500 into $17,000 playing craps at the Sands.

I learned how things operated from guys like Joe, and Pete Cigars, and Skinny Vinnie, and Vinnie the Bear, and Tony Bags, and the other men who were knocking around town when I got there.

It wasn't about having a lot of money. It was about handling your money right.

Like my friend Kip Addotta says, "How you handle your money is a big part of being a goomba. You tip the bartender, the maître d', and the waiter. Everybody gets a little piece of the action. And in return, you get treated like an *emperor*. And for what? For a few dollars!"

Kip is a very funny comic who I met way back when I was a bouncer. Later, he helped me with my acting career, and I was able to get him work at the Riviera. He reminded me recently about the tipping scene in *Goodfellas*.

Robert De Niro and his crew have just hijacked a truck. They've got their guns on the truck driver. De Niro takes the guy's wallet and pulls out his driver's license. He says, "You might know who we are, but we *know* who you are." He puts the guy's driver's license in his pocket. And then he gives him a couple hundred bucks!

As Kip says, "That was a very goomba thing to do—a very gentlemanly thing to do. The goomba is like a big Italian *mensch*. He does the right thing."

Even when the tipping thing looks complicated, it isn't. Here are more examples.

GOOMBA TIPPING DOS AND DON'TS

DO: Tip the maid.
DON'T: Tip the made guy.

DO: Tip the maître d' for a better table.
DON'T: Tip the doctor for a better operating table.

DO: Tip the D.J.
DON'T: Tip the D.A.

DO: Tip the guy who delivers the paper.
DON'T: Tip the guy who delivers the subpoena.

The place I grew up wasn't rough, exactly, but it wasn't too gen-
teel, either. My family's house was solid middle-class Italian. Same
with most of the guys I knew. One family bought their house in
1960 for $22,000. They just sold it for $640,000. A Chinese family bought it, or a Russian family. You hear people complain about
that—like it's some sort of invasion. Well, who's selling the
houses? It's all the Italians. So what are they angry at the Chinese
for?

It was a small-minded neighborhood in a lot of ways. People
thought Brooklyn was the center of the universe. They'd hear
about someone living in Manhattan and say, "It's so dirty. You're
living with black people there." Or they'd hear about some guy
moving to Manhattan and say, "I didn't even know he was a fag."
Like, what *other* kind of guy would move to Manhattan? That's
how little they knew.

When I'm back in the neighborhood now, I get all kinds of reac-
tions. Mostly people are proud, like I made a little something of
myself and that makes them feel good. Other guys give me a hard
time. They say, "Hey, look who's here—the big TV star. He lives
in Las Vegas now. He never comes around no more. He's on TV,
but no one sees him no more." It's ridiculous, actually. I'm around
there all the time. Maybe these guys have been in the joint so long
they haven't seen me visit.

Not much has changed for some of those guys since we were
kids. You see them on the sidewalk, like they were always on the

sidewalk. They're wearing jeans and T-shirts, and running shoes, and baseball caps. They dress exactly like they did thirty years ago, only now they got mustaches and, some of them, tattoos. Some of them still live with their moms.

That's where I came from. So I didn't start out in life with very high expectations, and I didn't start out very sophisticated about living the good life.

Now, I feel like I'm sitting on top of the world, and the best part is I know I could go back to anyplace I've been in my whole life and be just as happy there as I am here. It's all a matter of attitude. It's all about living the Goomba Diet!

CHAPTER 7

On the Diet,
Out with the Boys

There's nothing more important to me than friends. After family, that's it. My idea of a perfect evening is a good meal and a bottle of wine with my wife, my kids, and a few close friends. Most of the time, I like to pick up the tab. My motto is, If I like you enough to go out with you, I like you enough to pick up the tab. I enjoy taking a friend out to dinner. I enjoy being the guy who pays.

This isn't always easy. Sometimes a goomba will fight you over the check. It's a matter of pride.

It's also partly, I have to admit, selfish. I like to pay because that way I can eat and drink what I want. I don't want to think, "I'd like the lobster but he's paying so I'll get the chicken." I happen to like a $50 bottle of wine. To some guys, that's a lot. To other guys, that's a little. Whatever. The point is I wouldn't want to drink something I don't like just because the other guy is paying.

I like to be in control there. But more than that, I like to splash it around when I'm going out. I like doing it right. Just like with everything else, if I'm going out, I'm going *all* out. I don't see any point in doing it halfway.

Not all goombas are like this, of course. And not all people are goombas. Here's a quick check, in case you're still not sure about yourself or someone you know:

YOU MIGHT BE A GOOMBA IF . . .

- You think the show *Elimidate* is about somebody getting whacked.
- Your idea of *Extreme Makeover* is beating a guy until he's unrecognizable.
- When you get an eye exam, you tell the doctor, "I didn't see nothin'."

YOU MIGHT *NOT* BE A GOOMBA IF . . .

- You've ever gotten wasted on Manischewitz.
- You want your daughter to grow up to be just like Paris Hilton.
- You own an RV.

The guys I've known the longest are the guys I've known the best. They were there when everything important happened to me—good and bad. They were around when I lost my virginity, when I got drunk for the first time, when I made it on the basketball team, all the way up to when I got hired on *The Sopranos*. We stood on the corner together when we were kids trying to pick up girls. We stood together at the funerals after 9/11, when some of our friends were killed. These are real friends.

One way I know they're real friends is they've always been there for me when something bad was going on, and—this is more important—they were always happy for me when something good happened. That's not always true. Some guys, you know how it is. They're jealous. They say, "Why do you get all the lucky breaks?"

When I talk to these guys, it's like we speak a special language. I got one friend who calls me Stinky. I could explain that, but I don't have to. I got another friend who, when he calls me on the phone, I answer, "Juice. Go." I could explain that, too, but I don't have to. I've got friends who, if you heard me talk to them, you'd think we weren't actually communicating. I had this conversation with my friend Johnny Boy not long ago. Johnny Boy, a friend from my childhood, still lives in the old neighborhood and sees all the old gang. That morning, he had organized his usual Sunday softball game when I ran into him on the street.

"It's Sunday."

"Yeah."

"And?"

"Whatta you think? It was great."

"Who came?"

"Everybody. Cap. Richie Gitchie. Spotty. Yack. Vito."

"What Vito?"

"Vito Neck."

"What happened to the other Vito?"

"The other Vito—Vito Whatshisname—he didn't come."

"The Greek?"

"The Greek."

When Johnny and I were kids we had all kinds of adventures. Since there wasn't that much to do and we didn't have any money, we got into trouble. We had all kinds of ways to make extra money. One of them was stealing stuff.

There was a guy down the block who would buy things that we stole. He was actually a teacher at the school, but like everybody else he had a little thing going on the side. I guess he was a fence. We'd bounce around and steal things, and he'd buy them from us.

For example, he had a market for telephones. I have no idea who would buy them. But I know where he got them. We'd see one of those vans from the phone company parked on the street. A phone repairman would be in someone's house, trying to fix the phone, or he'd be up on the pole, trying to fix the line. Either way, the van was usually not locked. Why would you lock it? Who's going to steal a phone?

Us. We'd reach in the back and grab a couple of phones and run. The schoolteacher would give us five bucks apiece for them.

He liked to buy tools, too. Again, I have no idea what he did with them. But I know where he got them. We'd see a guy working on his car, lying on his back under the engine. We'd wait until he had to go into the house to get a beer or use the bathroom. You know he's not going to lock up his tools every time he goes into the house to take a leak. So we'd wait, and then we'd run and grab his toolbox.

Hubcaps were more valuable. Especially Cadillac hubcaps. You could get $50 apiece for those babies. That was a lot of money to me when I was seventeen or eighteen. Fifty dollars could by a lot of Spumoni Gardens' pizza. It could buy a lot of polyester disco shirts.

My friend Bo and I would go out looking for hubcaps. He'd drive and I'd scout. We carried a couple of tire irons. When we'd see the hubcaps, we'd pop them off with the tire irons and run back to the car. We grabbed a couple of sets and sold them. We were making a fortune! But we were greedy, so we wanted more.

One night we were in Brooklyn. It was late—after two o'clock in the morning. And we pulled up on this car, double-parked, in the middle of the street. It was a Cadillac, with all four hubcaps. It was a gold mine.

Bo parked his car in front of the Caddy. I got out with the tire iron in my hand. I bent down and was just starting to pry the hub cap off when Bo happened to glance in the rearview mirror. There was a guy coming up behind me with a baseball bat. He had the bat up like he was getting ready to swing. Bo yelled, "Stevie! Let's go!"

I jumped up and started running. Bo got the car started and the door open. I jumped in and we peeled out.

And the guy behind us dropped to one knee and started shooting. It was a setup. Maybe we'd already stolen the guy's hubcaps on an earlier raid. Maybe we'd stolen them more than once, from the same guy. He didn't want it to happen again, so he set a trap for us—and we walked right into it. Looking back, I think the guy was going to kill us. He was going to beat us with the bat and shoot us right there in the street.

We didn't steal any more hubcaps after that.

These days, I have more appropriate ways of having fun with my friends. We aren't criminals anymore. We have more fun than we used to, too.

Since a lot of hanging out with your goomba friends includes food, the goomba on the Goomba Diet is going to have to be careful in social situations. You don't want to spoil the party, but you don't want to go wild, either. If you're out with the boys, the boys are going to be saying, "Have another slice," or, "Have another steak," or, "Whatta you mean you've had enough?" You don't want to be rude, but there's limits. Remember: You drink too much tonight, you're not going to be able to drink at all tomorrow.

So here are some suggestions for how to decline without being offensive:

JUST SAY NO, THE GOOMBA DIET WAY
- "No more for me. I had *sfuyadell'* for breakfast."
- "No thanks. I'm going to have sex tonight, and I need to see what I'm doing."
- "That's all for me. I'm going to Yankee tryouts tomorrow."
- "I can't. I'm the designated driver."

No one will believe those last two—or even those last three—but it might distract the guys long enough to get them off your back.

Don't get the wrong idea. There's more to goomba life than just eating and drinking and sex. When goombas get together, they do all kinds of things that don't include food or booze or broads.

Here are some of them:

THINGS YOU'LL ALWAYS SEE GOOMBAS DOING TOGETHER
- Going to a ball game.
- Going to the fights.
- Buying leather jackets off the back of a truck.
- Laying down a bet at the track.

THINGS YOU'LL NEVER SEE GOOMBAS DOING TOGETHER
- Going to a yoga class.
- Going to a nail salon.
- Getting matching haircuts.
- Line dancing.

Ever since *The Sopranos* got popular, I get invited to go places. Not just me. The whole cast. We get invited to come to a restaurant, or a fund-raiser, or a private party, to make a personal appearance. This brings attention to the restaurant, and it can help raise money for a special cause. Believe it or not, people will actually pay money to hang out with me. People will bid large sums of money for the honor of having lunch or dinner with me and some of the guys from the show.

Sometimes I take somebody with me. When we get invited to go to the opening of a new casino, for example, we're always invited along with our wives. My wife isn't that big a casino fan, so sometimes I take a friend.

So—I took my friend Johnny Boy to this casino where me and a bunch of the guys from the show were making an appearance.

Two goombas we're proud of. Cap, who's a pharmacist, and former mayor Rudy Giuliani.

Now, Johnny's no kid, and he's been around the block a few times, but this was really special for him. Going to a high-class casino, staying in a high-class hotel, eating high-class meals—he loves all that stuff. Johnny Boy's been married a couple of times. He's got a couple of kids. So he's got a lot of expenses. He's not broke or anything, but he's gotta watch his money. So it's exciting for him to go all out on someone else's nickel. He really knows how to have a good time, and it's a pleasure to take him along.

I got invited to the Borgata, in Atlantic City, and Johnny Boy came with me. The limo picked me up first, and then we went to his place, right in the neighborhood. Since it would be a long drive ahead, we went to the Ravioli Fair to get something to eat on the way up. We got mozzarella and prosciutto and sandwiches. We had olives, stuffed with garlic, and some stuffed peppers, and some rice balls.

When we got to the Borgata, it was dinnertime. So we ate in the most expensive restaurant. I encouraged Johnny to enjoy himself.

Steve and Johnny Boy hanging out in the neighborhood.

He started with the shrimp cocktail and then had the biggest steak on the menu. The next meal, he had the lobster.

For guys where I came from, this is pretty big stuff. Remember, we grew up eating mozzarella sandwiches. That was a *good* meal, in those days. So if we get steak and lobster, we're in heaven. Does it taste better when you're not even paying for it? Yeah, maybe.

It's not just the casinos. HBO throws these incredible premiere parties for *The Sopranos*. The first year, we were nobodies, so the party was held at John's Pizzeria. It was pizza and draft beer. The next year, it was held at the Ziegfeld Theater—a step up. The next year, it was another step up, to the Roseland Ballroom. We had a big band and dancing. The next year, it was the Hilton Hotel, with the premiere at Radio City Music Hall. The next year it was Radio City Music Hall again, but this time the party was at Rockefeller Center—right down there in the middle, where they freeze it over in the winter for ice skating.

It was a gigantic party. The center was filled with these huge round tables. I brought along some guys I grew up with, guys from my building, friends, wives of friends, my mother. I got twenty-four tickets and took a bunch of people.

Most of these guys had never seen anything like it. Me, I'd been in Vegas awhile. Even if I wasn't always at the front table, I had seen some fancy stuff. These other guys? Forget it. It was like we'd all died and gone to Radio City Heaven. The food was incredible.

Maybe the nicest thing is, these guys still treat me the same way they did when we were kids. There's no airs. There's no attitudes. There's no jealousy. These guys are all excited for me, and they're all excited to be part of the premiere. I mean, they got to walk down the red carpet at Radio City Music Hall! But when it was over, nobody was giving me a hard time about how come I don't invite them more often or how about a loan or how about getting them a part on the show.

Maybe that's because I'm not different. I still act like the guy I was when I was young. That's the deal with me. What you see, that's what you get. I say what I say. I do what I do. I'm not laying it on for anybody.

Back in the eighties, when I first went out to Las Vegas, my mentor was a maître d' named Charles Najjar. He was smooth, elegant, and everything a Las Vegas guy ought to be. He wasn't a "player." He wasn't one of these loudmouthed goombas who's throwing money all over, flashing the big bankroll and the big pinkie ring and bossing everybody around—even though you see plenty of those. He had a nice quiet way of getting things done. He said, "It's easy to embarrass people into giving you money, but don't do it. Make a guy feel good about it. Never make a guy reluctant to give you money. Let him feel good about being a big shot and paying a little extra for something special." That was good advice.

He also knew the town better than anybody. I learned a lot from him. For one thing, he taught me how to have a good time.

In those days, he and three friends would make a night on the town. First, they'd call up three call girls—high-class, model-quality, beautiful girls, not hookers—and ask them for a date. This wasn't a date like they were hiring the girls, but a date like they were taking them out. Then, they'd pool their money. They'd throw in $500 apiece, which, in the late 1970s, was a lot of money. That was going to cover everything—drinks, dinner, parking, shows, tips, the whole thing.

They spared no expense. They'd have dinner at Chateau Vegas, the most expensive restaurant in town at the time. They'd go see Sinatra, the biggest show in town at the time. They'd tip the maître d' a hundred bucks to get the best table, and they'd sit right up front.

Afterward, they'd go to Jubilation. They'd go to a lounge. They'd been drinking wine and champagne and cocktails. They'd had so much to eat they were gonna bust. They'd seen the best show in town.

At the end of the night, if there was any money left, they'd take a shot. They'd take $200 and drop it on the roulette table, or lay it all on the line at a craps table. If they hit, it paid for the whole evening. If they didn't hit—hey, they'd already pooled all the money at the beginning of the evening, and had the time of their lives, so who cares?

That's a goomba way to live. That's really doing it right. When I was a young goomba in Vegas, I used to do the same thing, in a smaller way. I didn't have the money to get three friends and three high-class call girls and go see Sinatra after dinner at Chateau Vegas, but I tried to copy the spirit of the thing. After a long night out, me and my friend Vinnie would take a shot on the way out. We'd lay it all on the line, see what happened. Sometimes it paid for the whole night.

When we'd go out drinking, we'd lay all the money on the bar. We'd be twenty guys together, and we'd throw it all down there. There'd be $400, right there. Every time you'd order a round, some cash would come off the bar. We'd agree to keep drinking until it was all gone, no matter how long it took.

I'm not proud of it, but once or twice, I gotta admit, when things were tight for me, I took advantage of the situation. Me and the guys would go into a place where I had been running a tab. I'd grab some of the money off the bar and say to the bartender, "Take care of my bill, will you?" So the guys were helping me out, without exactly knowing it.

If you ever see a group of guys like that in a bar, and you're not sure whether they're goombas or not, listen to how they talk. These examples will help you decide:

THINGS YOU'LL NEVER HEAR A GOOMBA SAY

- "I love the design of the new Kia."
- "I'm gonna open a can of Whoop-Ass on you."
- "Could we have some more of the green salsa, please?"
- *"Café crème, s'il vous plaît."*
- "I want a side order of chitlins."
- "I find the Pinot Grigio more full-bodied than the Zinfandel."

As we've already seen, sex is a big part of the Goomba Diet. Without love and romance, the goomba is miserable. If he's miserable, he's eating. If he's eating, he could be overeating. If he's overeating, he could get fat. If he gets fat, hey, how's he gonna get laid then?

Sex is a big part of the goomba life anyway. If a bunch of goombas are out together, it's a big part of what the guys talk about. This is a goomba thing. If a guy is dating somebody, you're gonna know about it. If he got laid last night, you're gonna know about it. If he's having problems getting laid, you're gonna know about that, too. The goombas aren't like the WASP guys that way, where everything is a secret. The goombas don't have anything to be ashamed of. They're open about it.

I have a friend, a guy I grew up with, who everybody calls Jimmy the Horse. Why? He's hung like a horse. Since junior high school, everybody who knows him knows that. Nobody smirks or giggles when they say it. It's just his name, like he'd be called Jimmy the Nose if he had a big nose or Jimmy the Head if he had a giant head.

Another guy I know, he came out to Vegas. I was driving him somewhere and he said we needed to stop at a drugstore for rubbers. We got inside and he spent forever looking around. Finally I said, "What's the problem?"

He said, "I can't find my size."

"What size?"

"I need the extra-large."

I started laughing. I said, "What? You got a big cock?"

He shrugged. "Eh, I do all right."

Because guys talk about everything they do, I know a lot about sex. I know a lot about what my friends are up to in the sex department.

I know one guy, for example, whose rule is "No civilians." He might fool around—in fact, he does fool around, a lot—but never with a non-professional.

He'll go with a call girl or a hooker. He'll go to a whorehouse or a massage parlor. What he won't do is pick up some girl in some bar and take his chances.

I know another guy who goes to a place in Manhattan. It's a massage parlor, and they give you a real massage. You lie face-down and, for $90, you get the whole treatment. Then, at the end, the girl says, "You like?" If you say yes, she turns you over and you get the "Happy Ending" treatment. For another $30.

I know another guy who goes to a joint in New Jersey where you get a massage from five women at once. They wash you and scrub you and give you the rubdown. And it ends the same way, if you want.

I know several guys who have a wife and kids and also a girl-friend on the side. Some of them have had the same *goomada* for years. They're very careful not to get caught. They don't want to hurt anybody's feelings. They want to make everybody happy—including themselves. (In fact, I know one goomba who was so worried about blurting out the wrong woman's name at night that he got a *goomada* with the same name as his wife. That way, no matter who he's with, he's safe.)

Keeping everybody happy means living by the rules. So here are some more Goomba Diet rules for the guy who needs a little side order in addition to the entree:

MORE *GOOMADA* DOS AND DON'TS

DO: Introduce the *goomar* to your friends.
DON'T: Introduce the *goomar* to your mother.

DO: Take the *goomar* to your favorite restaurant.
DON'T: Take the *goomar* home with you after dinner.

DO: Try to celebrate Valentine's Day with your *goomar.*
DON'T: Try to celebrate Valentine's Day *on* Valentine's Day with your *goomar.*

DO: Give the *goomar* the occasional piece of jewelry.
DON'T: Tell her, "I bought it for my wife. She hates it."

I'm friends with guys I've known since elementary school. I'm friend with guys I met the first month I was in Las Vegas. I'm friends with guys from *The Sopranos.* And I'm friends with peo-ple who, to tell you the truth, I don't really know what they do for a living. It's none of my business. I'm not friends with this guy because he's an actor, or this guy because he's rich, or this guy because he's a powerful agent. I'm friends with guys because I like hanging out with them. So if a guy does something for a living that other people find questionable, that's their problem, not mine.

A friend of mine recently got indicted for some stuff involving some money that maybe he didn't earn in the usual way. Some people, who know that I'm friends with this guy, said, "Watch out, Steve. If people know you know this guy, they're going to want to talk to you."

They're welcome to come talk to me. If I'm friends with a guy, I'm friends with a guy. I don't care what he does for a living. It wasn't my business before, and it's not my business now. I didn't talk to him about how he makes his money. Why would I talk to *you* about it? I got nothing to say.

Loyalty is a big thing with the goomba, and it's a big part of the Goomba Diet. If I'm a guy's friend, I'm his friend all the way. There's no half-a-friendship with me. Same with most goombas. If you're his friend, you're going to have to do something pretty bad to stop being his friend. And I don't mean something illegal.

Maybe that's why I have so many friends. I don't ask anything from them except their friendship. That's all I want my friends to want from me. No favors. No handouts. No special treatment. Just my friendship. The guys that I'm close to know they could call me at three o'clock in the morning, no matter what the problem is, and I'm outta bed and on my way. They know that anything I have is theirs for the asking.

That's the Goomba Diet policy on friendship, the secret to strong friendships that last a long time.

CHAPTER 8

Sticking to the Diet Through Thick and Thin

A great celebration: Bobby and Carly's wedding.

Goombas are very big on celebrations. We celebrate everything. Somebody got a new job? Let's go out to dinner! Somebody got engaged? Let's go out to dinner! Somebody's moving into a new house? Let's have a party!

You celebrate good news and bad news. If a friend gets a divorce, you get some of the guys together and you go eat. If a friend gets fired, you get some of the guys together and you go eat. You're not celebrating, exactly, but you still want to have a good time.

On *The Sopranos,* we used to have a special dinner at Il Cortile anytime one of the cast members got whacked. We had big dinners for Joe Pantoliano, who got killed in season four, and for John Fiore and Jason Cerbone, who got killed in season three. Unfortunately the press got wise to this little tradition. By the time Drea de Matteo got whacked, the dinner was being held in an undisclosed location.

As you can imagine, all this going out poses a real challenge to the goomba waistline. Since there's always some good news or bad news to celebrate, the goomba could be eating out seven nights a week, plus the occasional lunch here and there. It's a dilemma. You can't not go—that would be insulting to your friend. And if you go, you can't not eat—that would be insulting to the other guys, and to the restaurant. And if you eat, you can't not eat right—that would be insulting to *you*.

So this gives the goomba an opportunity to practice restraint and moderation. In practical terms, this means not eating quite so much, but doing it discreetly. Here are some tips that will help you have a good time and a good meal, even if it's your fifth dinner out in a row, without having a heart attack before you finish dessert.

GOOMBA DIET HINTS FOR EATING OUT LIGHT

- Order a martini without the olive.
- Burn off extra calories by using your hands more when you talk.
- Don't order so much. Instead of having the salad, the soup, the bread, a pasta dish, a meat dish, and a dessert, eliminate something. Like the salad.
- Ask if you can order something off the child's menu. Just kidding.

Whatever you do, take it easy. Don't get carried away. If you eat too much, remember, you're going to have to go on a *real* diet. That will be bad for you and all the people who want to spend time with you—your family, your friends, your bartender, your waiter, and your maître d'. Imagine what would happen to the economy if all the goombas in New York suddenly said, "I ate out three times already this week. I'm staying home and having Weight Watchers." You'd put a thousand waiters out of work. Do you want that on your conscience? Of course not. So, *mangia,* but take it easy.

My mom and dad's goomba wedding. Doesn't everybody look great?

THE GOOMBA DIET AND THE GOOMBA WEDDING

There are times when even the goomba who is committed to the Goomba Diet is going to have to break training. One of them is weddings.

There's no celebration like the goomba wedding. This is the place to take the "live large" part of the Goomba Diet and really have a ball.

Go out to places like the Excelsior or the Vanderbilt in Staten Island. You'll see what I mean. Any weekend night of the year, it's goomba wedding time. And it's unbelievable.

Sinatra music will be blaring onto the sidewalk when the bride and groom and the guests arrive in the limo. The buildings themselves look like a wedding cake on the outside and a palace on the inside—very elegant, with flocked red wallpaper, crystal chandeliers, and mirrored ceilings, with a slight Las Vegas touch.

If it's in a place like that, it's probably an Italian wedding. If you're not sure, there will be warning signs.

IT'S A GOOMBA WEDDING IF . . .

- The grandmothers are all under 4½ feet tall.
- The uncles refuse to be in the family photographs.
- There are federal agents in the parking lot writing down license plate numbers.

Some of these big catering halls are booked eighteen months in advance for a Saturday-night wedding, and twelve months for a Friday-night wedding. Expensive? Don't even think about it. The average goomba wedding at a joint like this is going to cost you $100,000 or more. But what you get for the money! This is going to be a night to remember.

It starts a year in advance. The wedding date is chosen—after the wedding hall is booked. The bride starts thinking about the dress. The money is already flowing.

The night of the big party, the bride is going to be wearing a custom-made gown. The bridesmaids will be wearing matching dresses. The groom and the groomsmen will never look this good again until their funerals. They will arrive in a fleet of stretch limousines.

When they get inside, the consuming begins. There's an open bar, of course, and lots of champagne is flowing. The food is ridiculous. During the first part of the evening, which is the "cocktail hour," there are at least twenty different foods on the buffet tables. There's meatballs and cheeses, and clams and mussels, and shrimp and lobster tail. There's five different kinds of macaroni. There's prosciutto and olives and mozzarella and cold cuts. There's a sushi bar. There's an oyster bar. Imagine two hundred to three hundred people lining up for oysters and lobster tail. The average goomba doesn't usually get free lobster tail, so he's going to eat his fill tonight. And this is just the appetizers.

Then comes the dinner. Most places put an appetizer on the

table. Then they bring some macaroni dish—lasagna, or linguine with clams, or penne *arrabbiata.* Then they've got the entrees. This ain't your typical rubber-chicken dinner, either. Some of the fancier places offer ten or eleven different choices of entrees, so each guest gets to order, just like in a restaurant. Have the veal parmigiana or the veal chop. Have a nice steak. How do you like that cooked? It's done to order, for three hundred guests.

Don't think you're finished eating. After dinner there's a dessert table. It's called the Venetian Hour. It's just as over the top as the cocktail hour and the dinner. There are tables of ice creams and cakes and pastries. There's a guy making ice cream sundaes. There's another guy making cotton candy. There's another guy making dessert crepes. There's another guy operating this chocolate waterfall, like a fountain of chocolate to put on top of your desserts.

Plus there's the wedding cake itself. It's as tall as the bride, or taller. I've been to weddings where there is a large enough cake for everyone at the wedding, all three hundred guests, to get a slice. That's a lot of cake.

For some weddings, there's even more. There's a breakfast table—like, if you've passed out from overeating during the wedding and now you're awake and you need to start the day again. There's a guy making omelettes and breakfast crepes. You could get a side of bacon, to go on top of the ice cream sundae you just finished, in case your heart is still beating and your arteries haven't closed.

This, my friends, is the goomba way. If you've been paying attention, and living your life according to the simple principles of the Goomba Diet, this is the time to really live it up. The groom is your best friend! He's going to get married only once in his life— you hope! So what are you going to do—lay back and not eat? Say no to the lobster? Say no to the champagne?

Think what an insult it would be to your friend, and his family, and his bride, and her family. Going to the wedding and not having a good time would be an insult to goombas everywhere.

If you're the goomba father, or the goomba father-in-law, you should be living it to the hilt, too. I know goomba fathers who started savings accounts to pay for their daughters' weddings the day their daughters were born. They may go into hock to pay for this thing. They're spending everything they got on this one huge party.

That's because, in the goomba community, this is the only time they're going to do this. It's not like the WASP thing, where if it doesn't work out, you can always marry someone else. The goombas think you should get married once, and stay married. This is the only chance you got to do it right—so you're going to do it big. It's a point of pride.

Either way, if you're the goomba host or the goomba guest, you should be living life to the fullest. When you're at a goomba wedding, don't hold back. Celebrate! And keep eating.

The bride and groom have hired a DJ for the early part of the evening, and of course they have a live band, too, so the music is going the whole time. (They've also hired a photographer, and a video camera crew, to record the whole event for posterity. For some weddings it looks like they're being covered by *60 Minutes*.) The guests are on the dance floor. They're all drinking, so the dancing gets a little wilder as the night goes on. There's a choreographed bit of business, when the bride dances with her father, and then with her new husband. There are special songs that have to go with this—"Daddy's Little Girl," always, is the first number.

The bride and groom and members of their family are seated at a raised table at one end of the room. And just like you saw in *The Godfather* or *Goodfellas,* at a certain point the guests will start to approach the bride and give her envelopes with money in them. The bride is carrying a silk bag, made to match her wedding dress. This is where she's going to store all these little envelopes as they arrive, tucking them away like a squirrel storing nuts.

Some nuts! This is the *a boost.* Everybody is going to bring an envelope with cash in it, to pay their respects and to help the young couple get started in life.

There are special cards you get for the *a boost.* The cards have a hole in the middle of them, so it's easy to see right away what denomination bill is inside by looking at whose face is on it. Hello, Mr. Franklin! It's a *hunge*.

For a wedding like that, you gotta figure the bride's father is paying at least $200 a head for the wedding. So you're gonna want to bring at least a couple of *hunge* for the *a boost*. Most people bring more. You want to be generous. It's all part of living a big life. You don't want to be cheap with other people, just like you don't want to be cheap with yourself.

Besides, the family might need the money. I've seen many a goomba wedding end with the bride and groom having to dip into the *a boost* to pay off the balance on the wedding hall.

In the old days, when the average goomba didn't have any money at all, they used to celebrate what were called football weddings. The couple would rent a hall of some kind, cover the floor with sawdust, ask a friend who played the accordion to come and be the band, buy as much bottled or keg beer as they could find, and invite as many people as the hall would hold. For a meal, they served sandwiches, usually Italian cold cuts on Italian bread, wrapped in wax paper or cellophane. This is where the "football wedding" got its name. When it was time to eat, someone would stand by the box where the sandwiches were all stored, and ask people what they wanted to eat. One guy would say, "Salami and cheese," and you'd grab one of them, cock your arm back, and throw the sandwich at him like it was a football. The room was so crowded, this was the only way to serve the meal.

Old guys today still talk about going to football weddings. They'll tell you those weddings were the best. I don't think so. I think the modern weddings are the best. I went to one recently for my friend Joe Soup.

You know him as Joe Gannascoli, from *The Sopranos*. He plays Vito Spatafore—the guy who whacked Jackie Aprile, his own cousin, in the third season. On the show he's a *fanook*. In real life, I should mention, he's not. He's straight, and he got married last summer.

A great looking couple, Diana and Joe Soup.

Joe's a goomba with a big appetite. He eats big, and drinks big, and does everything else big, too. So when he got married, he went all out. It might be the nicest wedding I've ever attended.

It looked like a *Sopranos* convention. All the guys showed up to give Joe their support. Jim Gandolfini was there, and Michael Imperioli. Also Vince Curatola, John Ventimiglia, and Dominic Chianese. Stevie Van Zandt and his wife Maureen were there. Robert Iler, who plays Tony Soprano's son A.J., was there. So was Bobby Funaro, who plays Eugene Pontecorvo. So was Tony Sirico, who plays Paulie Walnuts.

We got there in time to make a big table for ourselves. Me and Michael started splashing it out pretty fast. I could see it was a huge wedding—over three hundred people—and I could see the food and drink were going to be flowing pretty heavy. So I grabbed a waiter, straight off, and told him what my wife and I were drinking, and I said, "I'm sitting here, and my wife is sitting here. I don't want to see these glasses empty the whole night. Okay?" I gave him twenty bucks and he took care of me.

Does this goomba look Chinese?

Then I grabbed another waiter and I said, "That seafood table looks pretty good. Bring me and my wife a nice sample of stuff, will you?" I gave him twenty bucks, too. When he came back, I gave him another twenty and said, "Keep it coming."

The food was fabulous. I've never seen anything like it. For the appetizer table alone, they had clams, shrimp, cracked crab, oysters on the half shell, and lobster tail. And caviar. They had a Chinese guy in a Chinese outfit making dumplings and egg rolls and all that. There was another guy making blinis and serving them with Absolut vodka. There was an Italian guy with sausages and peppers and olives and cheeses and all that.

Plus, a special appetizer had been created especially for Joe—a foie gras mousse on toast points. Not for nothing, but I ignored that and went for the lobster tail and cracked crab.

This wedding was held at the Vanderbilt, on Staten Island, right on the boardwalk. Joe grew up in Bay Ridge, so this is his territory, and all his people came. It was black tie. The men looked very

Cocktail hour at Joe's wedding.

elegant. The women were all beautiful, too. But I never saw so many women with fake tits in my life. I said to my wife, "What do they got here, a guy selling tits out of the back of his car?"

One woman had even been in for a tit reduction. She said, "Steve, do you notice anything different about me?" I said, "Yeah. I liked 'em before, when they were bigger."

Some of the women were extra crispy—tanned liked they'd done it in an oven. It was easy to pick out the goomba wives. Whatever they're doing, it's too much. The tan is too dark. The hair is too big. The nails are too long. The dress is too tight. And guess what? I think it looks great!

There's nothing subtle or understated about the goomba broad. If she's going to get a suntan, she's going to make sure the whole world knows about it. Unfortunately, if she's got a big ass, the whole world is going to know about that, too.

Because Michael and I were throwing around twenties, the maître d' was all over us, the waiters were all over us. They were standing by, ready to bring us anything we wanted. Every time I looked up they were bringing over another plate of food.

Was this excessive? I don't think so.

First of all, you want what you want, and you ought to be willing to pay a little extra for it. We didn't want to stand on line and fight the crowds for the food, so we threw the guys a couple of bucks.

Second, me and a bunch of the other guys at the table actually worked in these catering halls when we were kids. I did, and Michael did, and John Ventimiglia. So we know how hard it is for

these kids. They're nice Italian kids from the neighborhood. If we're not going to take care of them, who are we going to take care of?

Third, it's what Stevie Van Zandt calls celebrity vig. (For you non-Italians out there, "vig" is short for "vigorish," which is slang for "interest." If you borrow money from a loan shark, you find out what the vig is—like, how much you are going to have to pay back every week until you

Stevie enjoying some pigs in a blanket.

pay off the loan. In this case, it's the interest you pay for being famous.) You may be a fair tipper, but God forbid you should ever short somebody. The tabloids will know about it in a heartbeat, and you'll get a reputation for being cheap. People will say, "He's got alligator arms—they don't reach all the way to his pockets."

This is the exact opposite of the Goomba Diet way of life. You're supposed to live big. So, you gotta tip big, too.

We all had a great time. We were all asked to speak, and we all broke Joe's balls—in a nice way. A bunch of guys from the show went up and sang, too. Vince Curatola sang. John Ventimiglia sang. Dominic Chianese sang. Beautiful.

There was lots of other music, too. Joe had hired the New York

Dominic has been on the Goomba Diet for years. See how good he looks?

Police Department bagpipers to play "Ave Maria" during the cocktail hour. Then there was the deejay. Then there was a two-person band called Black and White, who perform at that new restaurant, Baldoria's, that was opened by the people who own the legendary Rao's. Joe had also hired, believe it or not, an Andrea Bocelli look-alike and sound-alike, to sing opera. He's the blind Italian guy with the beard, beautiful singer, who does all that classical crap. This was for Joe's father, who loves opera. Joe told everyone he'd flown the guy in from Milano, special for the wedding. In fact, the guy lives in Staten Island, and he's about as Italian as a knockwurst. But it was beautiful. He had the beard, and he sang with his eyes closed.

When it was over, we handed over the *a boost*. I made sure it was a big one, because I know Joe just bought a house and he could use the money. Plus he's a good guy, plus it's been good having him on the show, plus I got to break his balls. I said, "Now that Joe's got a wife, he can finally get what he really wanted—a *goomar.*"

No, actually, I didn't say that, but I thought about it. Instead, I told him he had wonderful tits. Gandolfini told him he had married above his head. The other guys roasted him a little, too.

Joe had a smile on his face from ear to ear. He told me later that he had such a good time he almost forgot to eat.

Whether you're a goomba or not, you may not know the proper way to behave at a goomba wedding. Here are some tips on goomba wedding etiquette.

GOOMBA WEDDING DOS AND DON'TS

DO: Bring the *a boost.*
DON'T: Give a $25 gift certificate from Home Depot.

DO: Congratulate the groom on his lovely bride.
DON'T: Remind the groom that you slept with her in high school.

DO: Congratulate the father of the bride on the lovely wedding.
DON'T: Ask him if he's paying for it out of the union pension fund.

DO: Tell the bride she's beautiful.
DON'T: Tell the bride she's hardly showing.

DO: Compliment the bride on her bridesmaids.
DON'T: As they go down the aisle, say out loud, "Did her. . . . Did her. . . . Did her. . . ."

It's a complicated social event, the goomba wedding. No one knows the origins of the strange rules and regulations. Why do you bring the *a boost* but not a wedding gift? No one knows, but if you show up with a toaster, you're going to look like an idiot. And a cheapskate. Why does the first dance of the night always go to the bride and her father, to the tune of "Daddy's Little Girl"? No one knows, but if you cut in and yell at the band to play "Danny Boy," you're going to get a beating. Why does the groom take off the bride's garter and toss it into the crowd? No one knows, but if you throw back a pair of panties the bride left at your house, you're going to get killed.

So be careful. Don't make a fool of yourself. Here are some more tips:

MORE GOOMBA WEDDING DOS AND DON'TS

DO: Bring a date to the wedding.
DON'T: Bring the stripper from the groom's bachelor party.

DO: Kiss the bride.
DON'T: French-kiss the bride.

DO: Ask the groom where he's going on his honeymoon.
DON'T: Ask the groom if you can come, too.

DO: Make friends with the people at your table.
DON'T: Start a game of Texas Hold-Em during the ceremony.

THE GOOMBA DIET AND THE GOOMBA FUNERAL

The goomba, if you didn't know it by now, is a very emotional person. He may not wear his heart on his sleeve or watch *Oprah* every day, but he's got very powerful feelings. If you don't believe that, go to a goomba funeral.

There's people crying. There's people sobbing. There's people trying to throw themselves over the casket. There's people trying to throw themselves into the grave. It's dramatic, believe me.

And lavish, too. Like a funeral director friend of mine says, "Italian people are strange. They may not be able to afford a decent piece of meat their whole lives. But when they die . . . it's gotta be the best!"

There's a whole set of goomba rules and regulations for the occasion. A goomba funeral isn't like a WASP funeral or a Jewish funeral, any more than having dinner with a WASP family or a Jewish family is like having dinner with an Italian family. The goomba funeral is more complicated than that.

First of all, there's the funeral home and the viewings. Most funeral homes are like palaces for dead people. They're built from marble and glass. The carpets are four inches deep. The curtains are like velvet. The pictures on the wall look like they were stolen from the Vatican. You feel like you're *in* the Vatican, in fact, because it's very silent and all the guys you see walking around are dressed in black. The difference is they're American and they're all wearing beautiful thousand-dollar suits.

They should be, because the average goomba funeral—like the average goomba wedding—ain't for cheapskates. The average goomba funeral could run you $8,000 to $10,000 or more.

The location or the name of the funeral home will tell you a lot about the guy that died. When I was a kid, Scarpaci's on 86th Street was the big wise guy funeral home. If a guy was being laid out there, you had a clue that maybe he was connected. That usually meant it was going to be a huge funeral, because every wise guy who attended was bringing his crew with him.

When Uncle Vito dies, the funeral home van comes and gets him. The embalmer and the other funeral home guys make him look good. Then the viewings begin. Uncle Vito is going to be laid out, in his best suit, in a beautiful coffin, looking like a million bucks, for his friends and families to visit and say good-bye one last time.

It's a little like the goomba wedding. The Italians like to do it up big. But most of them are working people who live in apartments or small houses. They don't have a big space at home to hold a big party. The restaurants aren't big enough to hold all the people they know, because a goomba from the neighborhood knows *everybody*. So, when it's a wedding or a Sweet Sixteen, they hire a catering hall. When it's a death, they hire a funeral home.

Traditionally, the viewings are from two o'clock to five o'clock in the afternoon, and then from seven o'clock to nine o'clock in the evening. Goombas being goombas, this presents an immediate question. Are you going to the viewing before or after dinner? Are you going before *and* after dinner? Where are you going to eat dinner? Who are you going to eat with?

So right away the goomba funeral turns into a social event. As soon as you hear that Uncle Vito has died, you find out where the funeral home is and you start making dinner plans. You start making calls. "Are you eating before or after? You wanna meet at La Trattoria?"

This is where it gets complicated for the hefty goomba. This is where the Goomba Diet comes in handy.

The average goomba knows a thousand people. I look at my own example. I grew up on the streets of Brooklyn. I had a circle of thirty or forty friends. I had neighborhood friends, baseball friends, basketball friends, high school friends, and college friends. Then I moved to Las Vegas and met more people. Then I started working the casinos and met more people. Then I started booking comedy acts and met more people. Then I became an actor and started making movies, and met more people. Then I got on *The Sopranos,* and met even more people.

I know a lot of people. And almost all of them have parents. And almost all of their parents are old.

So, guess what? I go to a lot of funerals.

This is true for all the goombas I know. It's a sign of respect and compassion to go to a funeral. You go for the friend, for the family, and for the neighborhood. It helps keep the culture together.

That means, obviously, there's going to be some eating going on. Because each of these funerals comes with a meal. If the goomba's not careful, he could get carried away with the funeral dining and wind up having a weight problem. And we know nobody wants that to happen.

Traditionally, the immediate family might have a meal before and after the viewing. In the old days, they would do this for three days straight—that's how long the body would be at the funeral home for viewing. These days, no. It's one day, usually, or two. So you have to make your dinner plans right away.

The family is dressed in black, of course—especially the older women, and especially the wife or the mother. You don't see them wearing the veil so much anymore, like you did when I was a kid. This is probably because it gets in the way of the eating.

See, even for the immediate family, the high point of the day is going to be the meal. Between five o'clock and seven o'clock, the family will leave the funeral home—where they've been saying hello to old friends, sharing the terrible news with other family members, and staring at dead Uncle Vito—and go get a meal.

As usual with Italians, it's a festive affair. Never mind they have to go back to the funeral home and start crying all over again. For now, let's eat! You wouldn't know the big group over there at table fifteen has just come from a funeral home, except that some of them are dressed in black and some of the ladies look like they've been crying. The men look like that, too, but their makeup isn't running.

I was having lunch recently with a group of friends in Brooklyn, at a famous old joint called Bamonte's. This is the real deal. It's crowded at lunchtime. You look around, you see the authentic old goombas having lunch. They've got their hair slicked back and their shirts open. They got the gold necklaces and the gold bracelets and the gold watches. They all have beautiful winter tans and very busy eyes. What do they do for a living? You never ask. You don't want to know!

At one large table near the door there was a birthday party for an old broad who must have been eighty-five or ninety. She was sitting at the head of the table wearing a little plastic tiara and drooling on herself. There were fifteen or twenty people at her table, laughing and joking and passing around huge platters of food.

At another large table in the back of the room there was another large group. There were fifteen or twenty of them, too, and they were also joking and passing around big platters of food.

Great goomba friends after a great lunch at Bamonte's.

But it wasn't a birthday party. Three of the older women were dressed in black, and the woman sitting at the end of the table had obviously been crying her eyes out.

But that was the only difference between her table and the birthday party table. And, now that I think of it, *my* table. We were eating the veal chops and the baked clams. So were they. All three tables had a few bottles of red wine being passed around. The waiters kept coming to all three tables, bringing lasagna, bringing shrimp in lemon sauce, bringing broccoli rabe, bringing more bread. . . . Only a goomba expert could have told you that one table was a birthday party, one was a funeral party, and the other was just a bunch of goombas having lunch.

At the funeral home, you'll know it's a goomba funeral right away. You'll see the guys in dark suits and pinky rings, the broads with the big hair and the nails. You see the Cadillacs double-parked outside. Some funeral homes in Brooklyn do only Italian funerals.

So let's assume the Brooklyn funeral is for an Italian guy from the neighborhood. Inside, you're going to find hushed music playing. You're going to see large floral arrangements in the room where the viewing will be held. Once you get inside, you're going to see the casket at the front of the room, with the lid up. Italians all go for the open-casket thing. So you have to be prepared to see the deceased, maybe not looking too good, or maybe looking *too* good. The funeral home guys are masters with hair and makeup. Sometimes a dead guy looks better than he has in years.

You probably shouldn't say that out loud. Here is some more guidance on how to behave once you're inside:

GOOMBA FUNERAL DOS AND DON'TS

DO: Wear a black suit.
DON'T: Wear a black jogging suit.

DO: Offer your condolences to the widow.
DON'T: Ask her for a date.

DO: Touch the casket and whisper your final good-byes.
DON'T: Say, "Bon voyage!" or "I'll see you in hell!"

For some of the older broads, and for some of the single broads, the funeral and the viewings are a big social event. The old ladies may not get out all that much. They don't socialize like they used to. They might go out for dinner once a month with their son or daughter. They probably have espresso and cannoli once a week with the ladies from the neighborhood. They probably go to church pretty often, some of them every day. But they don't get invited to nice places too much anymore.

So today's a big day. They're going to get out a nice dress, and they're going to spend a lot of time on the makeup, and if they get enough advance notice they're even going to go to the beauty parlor and have their hair done. After all, even though she wasn't all that close to Uncle Vito, she knew him for sixty years—and everybody she's ever known is going to be at the viewings.

For the younger broads, it's all about meeting somebody. Unlike a wedding, where everybody brings a date, Uncle Vito's viewing at the funeral home is going to have some single guys. Maybe this one has had her eye on Uncle Vito's nephew Sal. She heard that Sal got divorced recently, but that his construction company business is doing extremely well. She always liked Sal, since high school. This is a great opportunity.

So just like her grandmother, she's going to get out a nice dress and spend a little extra time on the face, and she might also, if she's got time, visit the hairdresser or squeeze in a half hour at the tanning salon. She's going to show up with the nails out to here and the hair lacquered until it's like a rock and the skin glowing orange like it's radioactive. Her dress is tight. Her tits are jumping out of the top of it. She's ready to go. Never mind that it's a funeral. She ain't showing no disrespect. She's just on the make.

Since not everyone goes to goomba funerals regularly, here are some tips on funeral etiquette. You have to behave yourself, or you won't be invited back. So mind your p's and q's.

THINGS NOT TO SAY AT A GOOMBA FUNERAL

- "He looks happy. He must've died in bed with his *goomada*."
- "That's not his suit."
- "Do you guys validate for parking?"
- "I heard it's a rented casket."
- "Is it me, or did he just move?"

The undertaker's job at a goomba funeral is a complicated one. Not only has he got the hysterical family to deal with at the funeral itself, he also has to make all kinds of preparations. A lot of goombas want to be buried with something special.

My friend Andrew is a third-generation funeral home director. He's a very nice, gentle guy, but a real goomba, and he's been around dead people all his life. He's heard all the stories.

He's buried lots of guys with guns. Loaded guns, into the casket, tucked away, just in case. He's buried just as many guys with bottles of wine. You're dead, you're dead drunk, who knows. In goes the bottle.

One guy wanted his mother to be buried with a flashlight. With batteries. Right before they closed the casket, he told Andrew to turn on the flashlight. "She's always been afraid of the dark," he said. He was serious.

Another funeral director I know told me he buried a guy with five pounds of sausage. He was a butcher.

This funeral director says he's also buried guys with bottles of whiskey, Baggies of marijuana, and even vials of cocaine. Is that a party or what? Buried in a box, in the ground, doing lines and smoking joints!

Andrew has buried a lot of people with stuffed animals. One time, it was a stuffed bear that played a little song. Somehow it got turned on, right before the casket was going into the ground. Suddenly there's music coming from somewhere. You could see the grieving family looking around, like, "What the hell is that?" Andrew knew it was the little stuffed bear.

Italian people are very religious, but they're also very superstitious. That's why they throw all this stuff in there. They know about God and Jesus and the Trinity and heaven and hell and all that. They've been to church. They know the drill.

Still, you can't be too careful. What if the church is wrong— God forbid? My own father was buried with a copy of *The Racing Form.*

This is also why no Italian person is ever buried with a picture of a loved one, or a child. Never! There's an old superstition that taking a picture of someone into the grave means they will be the next to die. So even the most loving father of all time would never ask to be buried with a picture of his wife or his children.

There are all kinds of rituals. One of them is that after the funeral, on the way to the cemetery, the hearse drives by all the dead guy's favorite places. Everyone understands he's dead, but they want to give him one last look at his house, at his place of business, at his favorite restaurant or bar, and even, I have heard, his *goomar's* place.

Another ritual involves the flowers. A lot of people send flowers to a funeral home when they hear that someone has died. But only the immediate family can send the gigantic floral "heart" that will stand on a kind of easel next to the casket for the viewing. This is an honor reserved for the widow, or the widower, or the children.

But things can go wrong. Andrew remembers how, the day after this one goomba died, *two* hearts were delivered to the funeral home. Both hearts said, "Beloved Father." Turns out the guy had one wife and two kids in the neighborhood, and another wife and *three* kids in Jersey. The second wife and kids knew he had been married before, but the first family never knew about the second family. They found out the hard way.

The first wife told Andrew, at the funeral, "If I had known about all this, I would have had him cremated."

The families are very upset when someone dies, of course. They can get carried away. I've seen people crying hysterically, and screaming at the coffin, and throwing themselves at the coffin. One time I saw a fight.

This goomba was on his second marriage. This can get a little sticky, because during the funeral each of the family members is going to get invited to walk up to the coffin and pay their final respects. So there can be some delicate feelings. Who gets called first—the first wife or the second? Who gets called next—the oldest son from the first marriage or from the second?

In this case, before anybody's name could be called, the oldest daughter from the first marriage jumped up and started screaming. "I'm sorry, Daddy! I love you! I want to go with you!" Then she turned to the second wife and said, "Now what are you gonna say? You killed my father!" Then the oldest son from the first marriage jumped up and said, "You bitch! You weren't even with him when he died! You were at the bank emptying his account!"

Soon, I swear, both sides were throwing punches. The sons were throwing chairs. The dead man's eighty-seven-year-old mother was spitting on the second wife.

Finally it got quieted down. But on the way out of the funeral home the first wife said to the second wife, "If you show up at the church, I'll kill you."

She didn't show up.

Another time, Andrew told me, he almost buried the wrong guy. They were cleaning up this man, putting on a nice suit and making him handsome, when someone realized something was wrong with the paperwork. Andrew called the widow and asked her very politely if she could come down to the funeral home. She took one look and said, "That's not my Eddie."

It turned out that two guys named Edward Walters had died on the same day. They were about the same age. They had the same name. And they both died at the Veterans Administration hospital. Somehow the bodies had gotten mixed up.

Andrew tried to explain this to the widow. She was very understanding. She said, "Oh, well. These things happen."

That would never, never have happened with a goomba family. The bodies might have gotten switched. But the widow would never have said, "These things happen." She would have strangled the funeral director right there in front of her dead husband.

Like I said, the social hours at the funeral home are from two to five and from seven to nine. From five to seven? It's reserved for the *goomada.*

This is the understanding. The family stays away between five and seven. They go out to eat. And the *goomadas* come in.

My friend Andrew has seen the same kind of weeping and wailing and hysteria as with the widows. Remember, the guy that's died might have had the same goomada for twenty or thirty years. It's not that unusual. It's like a second marriage for some guys. The younger goomba might have one that he changes every once in a while. The older goomba is likely to stick close to the same one. He's old. He's not hitting the spots the way he used to. If he's met a nice girl that's really good to him, he's not going to let her go.

So the *goomar* comes in to pay her last respects. In some ways, this can be even more emotional than with the family. Because the *goomar* ain't going to the funeral. She's not going to be welcome at the cemetery. This really is good-bye for her. This is the end.

Sometimes, unfortunately, there's more than one *goomar* there. If the guy is a little younger, or a little more active, he might have more than one girlfriend. The funeral director isn't a traffic cop. He can't control everything. So there might be a little tension if more than one brokenhearted *goomada* shows up at the same time.

The funny thing is, since the dead goomba's friends know that he had a *goomar,* or more than one, and they know the *goomars* always come to view the body between five and seven, sometimes the guy's friends show up between five and seven, too. His friends know he was a knockaround guy. They know he had some broads in his life. Maybe they met one and she was really good-looking. So they're coming around just to see what's available. It's a great way to meet girls! You know they're going to show up. You know they're willing. You know they're not looking to get married. So why not?

Sometimes, if it's a big funeral, the *goomars* will show up there, too. Or they'll show up for the regular viewing. A guy I know, a wise guy, died not too long ago. I went to pay my respects. There were about six girls there. One of them was the *goomar*—or at least one of them—but I couldn't tell which one. All six of them were dressed in black, and all six of them looked like hookers. They had the hair and the makeup. The black dresses were cut too low, and too short, and the high heels were hooker high heels. And they were having a blast.

It was like a night out for these broads. What would you expect? They know the dead man was connected. He was powerful, and he had money. They know he's going to have friends who are connected, and powerful, and have money. They might meet somebody! It's like a dead-goomba dating service.

Unlike a goomba wedding, going to a funeral doesn't automatically mean bringing the *a boost*. But it might. It depends on the situation. You have to know something about the person who died. If you know the family isn't doing well, you want to help out. If a guy dies and leaves his family with nothing, you're going to throw in a couple of hundred dollars. Otherwise, you send a mass card or flowers.

Remember, the funeral is a big event. It's a big expense for the family. You're honored to be invited. So you show your respect, and your concern for the family, by bringing a little envelope of cash to help cover the expenses.

Here are some final suggestions. Remember there are grieving people here. You want to be sensitive to their pain. So, try to avoid these embarrassing scenarios:

GOOMBA FUNERAL ETIQUETTE
- Don't tip the priest.
- Don't say, "How about a shout-out for the makeup person?"
- Don't say to the family, "So what about the hundred bucks he owed me?"

CHAPTER 9

Goomba Holidays
and Other Celebrations

Every day is a holiday for the goomba who's living his life right. If you're going to have a real appetite for life, there's always something to celebrate the Goomba Diet Way.

That usually means a crowd. The goomba never does anything alone. You hardly ever see a single goomba hanging out by himself on a street corner. You hardly ever see a goomba drinking alone. Even the phrase "eating alone," in wise guy terms, is a kind of insult. When you say a guy is eating alone you mean he's getting greedy, not sharing with his friends, keeping everything for himself. A guy like that will soon be described by other wise guy expressions, such as "sleeping with the fishes," or "wearing cement overshoes."

As my friend Vinnie used to say, "People who eat alone, they choke."

So naturally you don't see goombas dining alone in restaurants very often.

That goes for holidays and special events, too. Even romantic ones. On Valentine's Day, go into a WASP neighborhood, and find a romantic little restaurant, and you'll see nothing inside but tables of WASP couples, huddled together, eating dinner and speaking WASP to each other.

Not the goomba. No thanks. The goomba's gonna make it a party. When we celebrate Valentine's Day, we do it right. We book a whole room in a restaurant, or a whole wing of a hotel, and a fleet of limousines, and get twenty or thirty couples together and we make it a party. We hire a band. We get the food catered. We order the flowers. We pick the wine. We dress up like it's something special. Then we surround ourselves with the people we love, the people we've always celebrated everything with, and we have a huge party.

I'm not saying there's anything wrong with a romantic dinner for two. But do you want to waste a holiday like Valentine's Day on just two people? Nah. You wanna do it right, you do it big!

This is true for all the holidays and celebrations. The goomba is always looking for a reason to have a party. For some occasions, it's a big party. The wedding, for example, is always preceded by an engagement party, a shower, or several showers, and a bachelor party. For the engagement party, and the showers, the guests bring gifts. For the bachelor party, the guests bring condoms. The engagement party is for everybody. The showers are for the girlfriends. The bachelor parties are for the goomba's guy friends. Me, I'm a very forward-thinking, liberal guy. But I don't think women should go to the bachelor parties. And I don't particularly want to go to the showers. I think it's good the way it is.

The engagement party is like a miniature wedding. It's going to be a big lunch or dinner in a catering hall. There's going to be a band or a DJ. There's going to be a huge amount of food and drink. The bride- and groom-to-be will sit together, but not on the dais, and the room will be about half divided between her friends and family and his friends and family. The bride will get to show off her ring. The groom will get his balls broke by his friends.

When it's over, they get down to business. The girls all meet at the shower and talk about wedding presents and wedding dresses and honeymoons and whether they're going to have children right away.

The guys all meet. They have a few drinks. They eat a big meal. They might watch a few porno movies. Then the stripper arrives and it's off to the races.

For different guys, different things happen. I've been to ones where the stripper comes and does her routine and the guys all clap and maybe stick a twenty-dollar bill or two in her G-string. Then everyone claps and the broad gets paid and she goes home.

I've been to other ones where the broad stays a little longer. I've been to ones where she's got a few friends with her. A friend of mine went to one in Los Angeles thrown by a guy in the porno movie business. He had *twenty* girls there—all of them porno actresses. This one was doing that one. These two were doing those two.

At Dominic's bachelor party, a good time was had by all.

It can get a little crazy. It starts off as a performance. After a while, though, it turns into a free-for-all. Before you know it, who's in the bedroom, who's on the couch, who's in the closet, who's on the kitchen floor . . . ? Not just the groom-to-be, either. I've been to ones where *everybody* gets a taste.

For the goomba who's got a really big appetite, this is another opportunity to go nuts. I have one friend who had *four* bachelor parties. I didn't go to any of them, so I don't know the whole story, but I heard.

He's a big gambler, so one of them was at the Kentucky Derby, with all his horse-racing buddies. A rich friend of his from down south set it up. He flew in twenty broads from Brazil. Fifty of the groom's friends were part of the action. It lasted for four days. No one saw the actual race.

That would be enough for most guys, but not this friend of mine. After he recovered from that one, he had another one, in Atlantic City, for all his northern gambling buddies. He rented a suite of rooms and had some local girls come in for the night. The party went on for two days.

But he wasn't finished. He was planning on going to Foxwoods, the big casino in Connecticut, anyway. So as long as he was going . . . he arranged to have another bachelor party up there, for all his Foxwoods gambling buddies. That one was just one broad and a handful of friends. It lasted only one night.

You'd think the last thing a guy would be able to do, after all that, is think about getting married. So my friend had one last fling, right before the wedding. He had a traditional bachelor party in New York, for all his friends from the neighborhood. This was very subdued. One girl. Twenty friends. One night. I have no idea what happened at that one. I was invited, but I was working and I couldn't go. I'm sure it was very touching.

I'm not saying the bachelor party thing is good, and I'm not saying it's bad. But it's a tradition, just as much as bringing the *a boost* is a tradition, or the bride at the wedding dancing with her father to "Daddy's Little Girl," or the groom pulling off the garter belt after the ceremony and throwing it to the crowd. It's been going on a long time. I know very old goombas who still talk about their bachelor parties—not in front of their wives, of course. The bachelor party is sacred. You *never* discuss the details of a bachelor party with anyone who wasn't there at the time.

Talk about "What happens in Vegas stays in Vegas." This stuff you take to the grave.

It seems like the tradition might be dying off a bit, like all traditions. I know plenty of guys who got married and never had a bachelor party at all. I didn't have one. For some guys, there's something a little corny and a little creepy about it. If I'm invited now, I say "thank you" and stay home.

Even if you've never been to a bachelor party, you've probably got a pretty good idea what goes on. You probably think the guys all get drunk, break each other's balls, eat greasy food, and watch some porno movies until some skanky broad shows up to take her clothes off and then do disgusting things to the groom-to-be and, maybe, all of his friends.

All right, so you've been to one.

In case you haven't, here's what to expect. As you can see, it's not as sleazy as you might imagine.

THINGS GOOMBAS WILL DO AT BACHELOR PARTIES
- Practice philanthropy, by making contributions to the stripper's college fund.
- Study finance, by making a spot inspection of the stripper's assets.
- Experiment with chemistry, by mixing drinks and raising their blood alcohol level.
- Experiment with genetics, by depositing their DNA all over the place.

So it's not as bad as it looks. But it doesn't mean that anything goes. There are guidelines. There are things you won't see at the bachelor party. For example:

THINGS GOOMBAS WON'T DO AT BACHELOR PARTIES

- Sing show tunes.
- Take photos to show their wives.
- Have ginseng tea, herbal tea, or Mr. T.
- Invite the priest.
- Ask the stripper, "Could you come to the house and teach my wife some of this stuff?"

As I understand it, the stripper is generally guaranteed a certain fee to show up. She might be an entrepreneur, like one of the contestants on Donald Trump's *The Apprentice*. In that case, she might try to earn a little extra, by performing extra duties. She might be rewarded for these extra duties with extra payments. It is my understanding that her earnings could be substantial, if she is a hard worker.

Here are some final ideas for goomba bachelor-party etiquette. Follow these simple rules and you can't go wrong:

GOOMBA BACHELOR-PARTY ETIQUETTE

DO: Participate in all the activities.
DON'T: Say, "This is stupid. Let's play Twister!"

DO: Let the groom go first, and encourage him to enjoy himself.
DON'T: Compliment him on his performance, or say, "Nice dick, man."

DO: Applaud when the stripper removes her thong and throws it at the crowd.
DON'T: Catch the thong and then try it on yourself.

DO: Shove a twenty-dollar bill in the stripper's underwear.
DON'T: Keep your hand down there until you come up with eighteen singles in change.

DO: Slip a *hunge* into the bachelor's jacket to help pay for the evening.
DON'T: Slip in a packet of five condoms with two missing.

DO: Tip the stripper.
DON'T: Ask her if she accepts Visa or Mastercard.
REALLY DON'T: Attempt to swipe your card anywhere on her body.

At the other end of the scale, the goomba is big on birthday parties. The child's first birthday party can be a very special occasion. Same with the Sweet Sixteen, if the goomba has a daughter, and the twenty-first birthday. Like I said before—any occasion! Let's have a party! We'll have some drinks, and book a place, and get some food. . . . Any occasion is a big occasion, if you do it right.

Goomba celebrations start early.

My daughter Ciara's seventh birthday. Is my wife nuts?

I've been to goomba first-birthday parties that were bigger affairs than some WASP weddings. I'm talking catering hall, with valet parking, and a live band, and a photographer and video team, and an MC, and an open bar, and food like you wouldn't believe. All for a kid's first birthday! The gifts are lavish. The *a boost* is just like for a wedding or a funeral. You gotta come with some cash. Never mind that the birthday boy or girl will never even remember the event. That doesn't matter. This is a big day in the goomba parent's life, and he wants to share it with all his friends and family. Imagine the pride of the grandparent when his or her first grandchild celebrates a first birthday. Imagine the pride of the guy who's just become an uncle for the first time, and now is celebrating little Frankie's first birthday. You can imagine what an event this is for the goomba.

Naturally enough, the party wouldn't look like a regular birthday party. Here are some ways of telling the difference between this and a regular kid's celebration.

IT'S A GOOMBA BIRTHDAY PARTY IF . . .

- You yell "Surprise!" and the birthday boy puts his hands up.
- You yell "Surprise!" and a stripper jumps out of the cake.
- There are pony rides, and all the uncles start laying down bets.
- The birthday boy won't say how old he is without a lawyer present.
- One of the birthday presents is a mortadella.
- It's a themed birthday party, but instead of Spider-Man or Harry Potter, it's the Godfather.
- There's a clown, but he keeps saying, "You think I'm funny? Do I *amuse* you?"

The Sweet Sixteen parties can be even more elaborate. I attended one last spring, and I was stunned. It was as big as some goomba weddings I've been to.

There were at least three hundred people there, almost all of them kids. The boys were wearing suits. The girls were wearing dresses. There was a DJ and a live band. The dinner was just as elaborate as it would be for a wedding. The appetizer tables were ridiculous—seafood and Chinese food and Italian food and everything. After dinner, there was a dessert section that was amazing. I saw one guy making ice cream sundaes, another guy making crepes, another guy making waffles, and another guy whose job was to pour chocolate sauce, off this chocolate fountain, onto ice cream sundaes and crepes and waffles and everything else. It looked like *Charlie and the Chocolate Factory.*

The birthday girl looked like a cross between Pippi Longstocking and Paris Hilton—half teenybopper and half hooker. She had so much hair and makeup, and her dress and her high heels gave her such a grown-up body, that I had a hard time believing she was sixteen.

She entered the party like royalty, coming up through the floor in a glass elevator, accompanied by these two hired hunks in tuxedoes. All her friends screamed and yelled. The camera bulbs flashed. The video team swooped in like they were covering the MTV Video Awards. The music started and the party was on.

The kids danced. The adults watched. Everybody ate. Everybody ate some more. There were little speeches. The girl's father got choked up, which is exactly what a proud goomba father should do at a time like this. The girl's mother sat at her table bawling her eyes out, which is exactly what a proud goomba-ette mother should do at a time like this. It was very touching, and it went on until way past midnight.

I found out later that the girl's father had spent $25,000 to launch his little darling into society. He was a plumber. He probably spent a third of his entire year's earnings on this one important evening.

Some people would say that's foolish. But that's the goomba way. I'm not saying every goomba dad should spent a third of his annual income on his daughter's Sweet Sixteen party. I'm not even sure the Sweet Sixteen party is such a good idea. But if the goomba is going to throw the party, he's going to go all the way and do it right. There's no holding back.

Remember, there is nothing worse for a goomba than being considered a cheapskate. You might need to be careful about throwing your money around, but throwing a party for your daughter ain't the time to do it.

If you're worried about being considered cheap, watch out for these warning signs.

YOU MIGHT HAVE ALLIGATOR ARMS IF . . .

- You tip waiters with food stamps.
- You own a jogging suit and actually exercise in it.
- You look for Blue Light Specials at Kmart, for an anniversary gift.
- You charge hookers on your credit card, for the miles.

Don't let anyone call you cheap. If you're in, you're all the way in. That's the goomba way.

In most goomba households, Christmas is a pretty big holiday. Of course that's true in non-goomba households, too. Everyone in America seems to celebrate Christmas. I have Jewish friends who do holiday lights and have a Christmas tree. They celebrate Hanukkah, then they celebrate Christmas, too. So how do you know if it's a goomba Christmas or not?

Here are some indicators:

IT'S A GOOMBA CHRISTMAS IF . . .
- Baby Jesus is visited by the Three Wise Guys.
- The goomba hangs the mistletoe from his belt.
- The goomba says, more than once, "I got your North Pole right here."
- The goomba tells his kids the presents "fell off the back of a sleigh."
- The goomba kids write Santa to ask for presents, and use the words "Or else . . ."

If you're passing by on the street, and you hear singing coming from the house, the music will help you decide. Are they singing the traditional Christmas songs? Or is there a goomba flavor to the music you hear?

Here are some indications it's a goomba Christmas party:

GOOMBA CHRISTMAS CAROLS
- "Oh Little Town of Bensonhurst"
- "Hark! The Herald Angels Sing (To the Feds)"
- "Cheech's Nuts Roasting on an Open Fire"
- "I'll Be Home for Christmas (If I Get Parole)"

- "Rudolf the Red-Nosed Consigliere"
- "(You Have the Right to Remain) Silent Night"

The problem for the average goomba, of course, is that the goomba Christmas is going to involve a lot of eating. How can a goomba stay on the Goomba Diet around the holidays? The same way he does the rest of the year. He's gonna take it easy and enjoy himself, eat everything he wants, and feel great about himself afterward. Simple.

In my family these days, Christmas is a big deal. My family is Italian. My wife's family is Mexican. Any way you slice it, that means a big Christmas. The house is very decorated. There's always a tree. There's always presents under the tree. On Christmas Eve there's always lots of people around and tons of food. It's my family and my wife's family, and her brother's family, and friends of ours and their kids, and anyone we know who doesn't have family. The food is a big part of it, of course. We have breaded shrimp, and sausage and peppers, and maybe a lasagna. My wife's family does Mexican dishes like flautas and guacamole and enchiladas. We'll have a chicken, potatoes and onions, a Caesar salad. . . . It goes on and on.

Santa comes, too. We have a guy who we've used for the last seven or eight years. He comes with an earpiece and a walkie-talkie. When the kids get on his lap, my wife starts feeding him information. Santa knows all the little children's names and all the little facts about them, and they are always stunned. He's a beautiful guy. I give him $100 for a half hour. He does about six or seven houses each Christmas Eve. My mother-in-law sits on his lap and I always accuse him of looking down her blouse.

When I was still a young guy, but had moved into my own place, Christmas Eve was always a party. Even when we had a small house, we'd still have seventy-five people over. It used to go on all night—until five in the morning, sometimes.

No matter where it was, or who was throwing it, the big thing about the Christmas party was always the food that went with it.

The staff at Rao's. Incredible meatballs.

The big event isn't the opening of the presents or the lighting of the tree. I'm sure that's all very nice, but for the goomba it's the traditional Christmas meal—the Feast of the Seven Fishes.

Why seven? It has something to do with the seven sacraments.

The important thing is that it means Christmas Eve dinner is going to be seven different kinds of delicious fish.

Every family does it different. Every combination of seven fishes is different. When I was a kid we didn't do the traditional Seven Fishes, but we did a variation on it. My father would cook his breaded shrimp—which I still cook to this day—and there would be baked clams, linguine with mussels, maybe something with *fra diavolo* sauce.

Some families just had ravioli or some other macaroni in lobster sauce. Some families didn't have either. Some families had squid. Some families had crab. But the basic idea was always the same. You ain't getting any chicken or steak. There's not going to be any ham or turkey until Christmas Day. On Christmas Eve, it's fish.

That means a beautiful linguine with clam sauce. It means baked mussels in marinara sauce. It means clams oreganata. It means shrimp in lemon sauce. It means baccala, in some families—

Mario Batali and our friend, Mary Beth Mazzotta.

the dry salty fish that I sort of got my name from on *The Sopranos*. It means some kind of big whole fish as the main course—sometimes a salmon, sometimes a flounder—usually stuffed, and usually baked.

It means a feast made up of things that, the rest of the year, the average goomba family can only dream about. All year long, the poor goombas have been eating nothing but macaroni in tomato sauce, with bread and maybe a little meat on the weekend. Sausages when you're lucky. A little roast from time to time. A steak, if things aren't too tight.

No matter how broke we were, though, Christmas Eve was the Feast of the Seven Fishes. There was no skimping here. There was no Filet-O-Fish from McDonald's. There was no Mrs. Paul's Frozen Fish Fingers. It was all calamar' and scungill' and the other special treats.

In places like New York, a lot of restaurants observe the holiday by serving the Feast of the Seven Fishes on Christmas Eve. Mario Batali's Babbo does a huge spread. So does Mario's place Esca. So does Gusto, in the Village. So does Patsy's, the joint on 56th Street where Frank Sinatra used to hold court.

After a meal like that, with a few glasses of wine thrown in, and a nice cannoli and Sambuca to finish it off, lying back in his easy chair, his belt buckle and the top of his pants undone—talk about sleeping with the fishes!—the goomba is going to be full of gratitude and Christmas spirit. Now he can get up on Christmas Day and really celebrate.

Thanksgiving can also be a pretty big deal in some goomba families, because—let's face it—it's mostly about food. There's no religion. There's no gift-giving. There's just cooking and eating.

Which is weird, because Thanksgiving is obviously not a holiday invented by the goombas. If it had been, the goombas would have started it when they came over with Columbus and the other Italians, around 1492, instead of waiting for the Pilgrims in 1620. There would have been no Plymouth Rock and all that; the goombas would have headed straight for Atlantic City. Thanksgiving would be celebrated on a Sunday, too, and not a Thursday night. Sunday is the night for holidays. Thursday is, like, poker night or something.

Besides, if they had been goomba Pilgrims, all the pictures of the first Thanksgiving would have shown the Pilgrims sitting around after dinner, loosening the belts on their pants *and* on their hats.

Thanksgiving is still one of my favorite holidays. It's all about eating and drinking and sitting around with people you like. There's not all the craziness you get at Christmas, with the gifts and all that. There's not all the decorating the house. It's just good people and good food.

A lot of food. You're going to have the antipasto tray, with the roasted peppers, mozzarella, Italian olives, maybe some anchovies. There's going to be the provolone, the soppressata, the salami, and maybe a tomato salad with onion. Of course there will be a nice Italian bread.

This is just appetizers. You might sit at the table for this, or eat it from a buffet. You probably take a little break, after that—sit on the sofa, have a rest and talk.

Then it's back to the table. There's going to be rice balls, maybe a lasagna, maybe some other macaroni. This is a big part of the meal.

After that, finally, here comes the traditional Thanksgiving meal. Here's the turkey and the dressing, and the ham, and the mashed potatoes, the roast carrots, and the sweet potatoes.

And, after that, at the end, there's the pumpkin pie. And also the cannoli. And maybe a *sfuyadell'*—a special Italian pastry I mentioned before called a *sfogliatelle*.

Stevie Van Zandt grew up with both meals, too. Since his father was Dutch, they had to have the traditional Thanksgiving meal. But since his mother was Italian, and since her mother was the cook in the family, they had to have a big Italian meal, too. Every Thanksgiving, there would be a turkey and what Stevie calls "all the *Amerigan* stuff," but there would also be his grandmother's specialty, Wedding Soup, which is a kind of chicken soup with meatballs in it, and the other Italian dishes.

The meal usually starts around two in the afternoon. It ends after five. When it's all over, if it's a typical goomba Thanksgiving, it's like they passed out Valium. Everyone is nodding off. Everyone is sitting on the sofa. The men take off their shoes and unbutton their pants. Half the people take a little nap.

And then, around seven or eight, after all the guests are gone and the place is all cleaned up, someone will say, "Who feels like having a little mashed potatoes and dressing?" You heat up some leftovers and you have a light dinner.

When I moved to Las Vegas and got married and bought a house, we used to throw these big Thanksgiving parties. I was working at the Riviera, and my wife and I would open our home to all the people who didn't have anyplace else to go. There were usually some comics who were working that weekend, and they couldn't get home for Thanksgiving, so we'd have them come to our house.

We'd usually have forty to fifty people. Some of the guests

My fortieth birthday. Hope I make it to fifty.

would bring pies or desserts. Some of them would bring booze. Sometimes they'd send flowers to my wife. And sometimes they'd bring nothing. I remember one comic showing up, year after year, and never bringing anything to my house—not even flowers for my wife. And every year, after dinner, he would ask for a doggie bag. I'm not going to say his name, but he knows who he is.

What is that? Someone goes to your house for Thanksgiving dinner, empty-handed, and when they leave they ask for a doggie bag?

We used to have huge parties all the time—not just on Thanksgiving. We'd have them catered, and we'd have valet parking. (For my fortieth birthday, we had more than 150 people. I remember we went through seventy bottles of champagne.)

After a while it started feeling out of control. I'd go to bed at three o'clock in the morning and then get up at nine to start getting ready for work. There would be people *still* at the party. We'd have people we didn't even know asking us about our next party. People would say things like, "You should have a party on Fourth of July." One time a woman asked us if she could throw her parents' wedding anniversary party at our house. At *our* house? I thought she was kidding.

We stopped throwing all those parties.

Fourth of July is a good time to have a cookout with friends. You get some sausages and peppers, a few steaks, and some illegal fireworks—you're there. Valentine's Day we covered. Halloween, even for the kids, isn't that big a deal. Who wants to put on a costume? What are you going to dress up as?

Mostly, these are just ordinary days.

Easter, though, is a big deal. Remember that most Italians are Catholics, or come from Catholic homes. Even if they're not regular churchgoers—I don't attend church services, even though my wife and children go for Easter, Palm Sunday, Christmas, and some other holidays—they turn Catholic again just in time for the holidays.

In my home, when I was a kid, we always had huge Sunday meals on Easter. It's the end of Lent, when everybody is supposed to give up certain foods or supposed to fast. (That never happened in my house, believe me.) To break the fast, a lot of families will make a roast lamb. There's a special bread, like an egg bread made with candied fruits and nuts. There is always a special ricotta pie.

In a different way, Columbus Day is a big holiday in the Italian community, too.

Anybody who knows his history knows that Christopher Columbus's real name was Colombo, and that he came from Genoa, Italy. So an Italian discovered America.

That's why Columbus Day is celebrated in cities where there are lots of Italians, and that's why the goomba makes it a special day. The schools are closed. There's a parade. The mayor goes out and tries to look Italian. He eats a sausage-and-pepper sandwich in

The famous Lucy, on 18th Avenue.

front of the photographers and tries to look like he's enjoying it.

Goombas are also really big on celebrating the feast days of the saints. Everybody's heard of the Festival of San Gennaro. If you've ever seen a movie about Italians in New York, you've seen the Festival of San Gennaro. Well, lots of little villages and neighborhoods have their own San Gennaro celebrations, except that the names are different. It's Santo Pietro or Santa Rosalia or whatever.

For the goomba, this is a golden opportunity to eat. The kiddies may like it for the rides. The older ladies like it because it means extra socializing time. The goombas like it because of the food.

The streets in the neighborhood will be lined with booths selling every kind of Italian specialty you can think of. Here's a booth with the sausages and peppers. Here's one with pizzas and calzones. Here's one with fresh cannoli. Here's one with the rice balls. You go from booth to booth, eating yourself to death.

It's a big tradition for some families to go every year—the ones who work at the festival, too. There's a great restaurant in

Brooklyn called Lucy's, run by a great broad named Lucy, naturally. She's famous for her Pinelli Special. Lucy cooks them herself, out of *ceci* beans, which are also called garbanzo beans, made into a thing that looks like a ravioli and gets deep-fried. She serves that with ricotta cheese on top and it's out of this world.

Her family has been serving that at the San Gennaro feast for seventy years—her grandmother, her mother, and now her. In addition to running her restaurant—it used to be down in Little Italy, on Mulberry Street, until she moved to Brooklyn a while back—she does all the festivals.

You've seen her stuff, even if you've never been to any of those feast-day celebrations. Lucy and her booth are so famous they've been in the movies. *The Godfather, Copland,* and *Witness to the Mob* are just a few of them.

Why wouldn't you put that stuff in a movie? It's colorful. It's noisy. It's a celebration. It's about eating and drinking. What's not to like?

CHAPTER 10

Being Famous on the Goomba Diet

The combination of six years on *The Sopranos* and two *Goomba* books, one "Goomba" young adult novel, and all the publicity that goes with it, has made me sort of famous. Not *famous* famous, like Brad Pitt, but just regular famous—like, people notice me, and they say, "Hey, aren't you the guy from that TV show?" Someone might say, "Hey, aren't you the guy from *The Sopranos*?" Some people know exactly who I am. They say, "Yo! Bobby!" like we were old friends from the neighborhood. They can recite lines from my scenes on the show.

Not always. I showed up for the first week of work last season and a production assistant stopped me as I was entering the studio. She said, "Excuse me, sir. Are you part of the production?" That'll knock you down a notch or two—when the P.A. for your own show doesn't know you.

Luckily I was already on the Goomba Diet. I was a happy guy before *The Sopranos* made me a little famous. I'm happy now. I'll

Me and my beautiful wife, Laura, on the red carpet.

be happy after *The Sopranos* is gone. I had already figured out that the secret is to be satisfied with what you got, and be hungry for just a little bit more.

It's just like eating. If you eat too much, you're not going to enjoy what you ate. If you have too much, you won't enjoy what you have. You should always have just a little less than you want.

When it comes to fame, maybe a little is better than a lot, anyway. I wouldn't want to be, like, Tom Cruise famous. Can you imagine? You'd have the paparazzi following you around, trying to catch you taking a dump or getting caught shoplifting. You'd have to walk down the red carpet and actually *talk* to Joan Rivers.

A little fame is good. Nice things happen to you. Here are some examples:

YOU KNOW YOU'RE A LITTLE BIT FAMOUS WHEN . . .

- Your local deli names a sandwich after you.
- You're on *The Tonight Show* but not in the "Jaywalking" segment.
- You're on *Dr. Phil* or *Maury Povich* but you're not a transvestite social worker who's in love with his/her own Siamese twin brother/sister.

Being a little famous is fine. You get extra attention. People smile when they see you, even if they can't remember where they

Me and my beautiful wife—oh wait, that's not me.

think they know you from. People send over drinks, or bottles of wine, and all they ask in return, most of the time, is a smile and an autograph.

You also get a lot of free food. Is this just an Italian thing? I don't know. When I'm in Brooklyn, I like to hit a few spots. I'll swing by the Ravioli Fair, or Spumoni Gardens, to pick up something for the family. But the minute I come through the door, it's "Hey, Steve," and some guy is handing me a slice of prosciutto or a hunk of provolone. "Have a sandwich, Steve!" I say, "I just ate." They say, "So have half a sandwich."

What are you gonna do? You can't say no. You can't insult the guy. So you take a few bites, and it's out of this world, and you tell the guy it's delicious. And of course he says, "You like that? Try the mozzarel'."

If you're not careful, you could eat lunch six times a day, just walking around. You'd have to abandon the Goomba Diet and go on a real diet. Horrible!

But the thing is, even though I like the free food, I don't like

A poor fat kid from Brooklyn. Is America a great country or what?

some of the stuff that goes with it. I like being treated like a celebrity, but I don't like being *around* celebrities.

I never know what to say, when I meet some famous person who, let's face it, the only reason I know them is they're famous. What do you say to, like, Sarah, the Duchess of York? "I love your work"? or "How's the Weight Watchers thing going?"

But there are a lot of famous people I'm happy to meet. Ted Danson is a big fan of the show. That was nice to hear. I met Steve Martin, and I said, "I'm a big fan of yours." He said, "No—I'm a big fan of *yours*." That was great. When I used to do *Hollywood Squares,* I met Dom DeLuise. Unbelievable. He's a hero of mine, from the movie *Fatso*—a great goomba movie. I used to hang around with Martin Mull, who's fantastic. I got to know Alec Baldwin.

What? You didn't know Mork was a goomba?

The Sopranos has been honored a lot at the Emmys, and I see a lot of guys there that I know. Here's Chris Rock, and Ray Romano, and David Spade. These are all guys that I know. I mean, I *know* know them. I don't just know them, like they're someone I met one time, or did a little work with. I mean, I've known them a long time, back to when I was booking talent for the comedy room at the Riviera Hotel in Las Vegas. I see these guys and they know I'm doing good, and they seem happy for me.

But it's a double-edged knife, being famous. You get bothered a lot, too. Sometimes a guy will say, "Hey! I love the show!" and that's great. Sometimes he'll ask for an autograph, too. That's fine. I don't mind that. Sometimes he'll ask for two autographs. Okay, it's a little pushy, but whatever. And sometimes he'll just be an asshole.

I was at a ball game recently with my wife. Some guy came over. He'd been drinking, but it's a ball game, so maybe he's just had a beer. He says, "Howya doin'? Listen, I got my girl on the phone. She doesn't believe it's really you. Would you please talk to her for a second?"

Bono. He sang a duet with Sinatra. That's good enough for me.

I said, "Sure." Then I got on the phone and said hello to his girlfriend. I figured, this is an easy way to get rid of the guy. It usually works, even if it's sort of obnoxious when they ask. You get guys saying, "Would you talk to my mom? She's sick in Jersey." I don't like that, but I'll do it. Even though sometimes it's stupid. You get people on the other end of the line who think it's a gag. "Who is this?" they say. "Oh, come on—you're not Bacala. That's not even his voice."

Anyway, this guy at the ball game comes back. Now, he's drunk. He's got the cell phone in his hand. He says, "Hey, man. This is my boss's sister on the phone."

I probably would've done it, just to make him go away. But my wife—she doesn't like it. She says, "Do you mind? We're trying to watch the game. He already talked to your girlfriend. Why don't you leave us alone?"

Now the guy's insulted. "Oh, I get it," he says. "Now you're a big TV star. Now you don't talk to normal people anymore."

The cell phone—and the cell phone *camera*—has changed

everything. Everywhere you go, someone has a phone and someone has a camera. You're in a restaurant, or a bar, and some drunk wants you to talk to his mother in Cincinnati. You don't want to be a jerk, but it gets pretty old. You can't win.

Sometimes being a little bit famous is a good thing. I was trying to get my daughters to their religion class a while ago. Somehow I went to the wrong place. We were wandering around and I couldn't get a cab, when these two cops stopped to say hello.

I said, "Hey, fellas. We're running late for something. Could you give us a lift?" So we got in the car and they drove us over to the church. I said to my daughters, "Take a good look. This is the last time you will *ever* be in the backseat of a police car."

I've also had the opportunity to use my small amount of fame to help people. I had a friend who was going to get married. He had the invitations printed and sent out. Everything was set. Then he got a call from the catering hall—they have to change the date. Apparently some high roller came in and offered more money for the room.

I told my friend, "You can't let yourself be treated like that. Tell the guy it's not happening."

But my friend was nervous. He said, "No. *You* tell him. Come with me."

So I went. I told the guy, in a very polite way, "This is a nice man. This is a nice couple. I know you want to do the right thing by them. I know you want to be nice, too, right?"

The guy freaked out. He was scared. He said, "What are you going to do to me? I feel like I'm on your TV show!"

I said, "Forget *The Sopranos*. This is like *The Wedding Planner*. You just gotta do the right thing here."

He did the right thing. My friend got married on the date it said on his invitation. And he got a nice rebate for his trouble. Partly because the catering hall guy got me mixed up with the character I play on TV.

Another guy could have done the same thing, but he might have needed to apply more pressure. My friend Johnny Boy got married years ago on Staten Island. He had a huge wedding—more than five hundred people. This was in the 1970s. The price tag was $12,000. But when it was over, the catering hall presented him with a bill for $16,000. He said, "What for?" They said, "You had some extras." He was furious. They had a deal—this many people, this much money, everything included. But they insisted.

So he asked his new brothers-in-law to go pay the guy a visit. They were very well known guys, and very tough. When it was over, Johnny Boy had a new bill. He only owed them $11,000. To this day, he says, "How they did that, I don't know. I don't *want* to know."

Like I said, when it comes to friendship, I'm on the Goomba Diet. I'm all the way in. I will do *anything* to help a friend.

But that's me, Steve Schirripa, helping a friend. All you have to do is ask, and I'm there. If you want Bobby "Bacala" Baccalieri to show up . . . that's different.

People spend a lot of money to hang out with Bacala. Literally. People spend big money just for the privilege of hanging out with this guy, and with the other characters from *The Sopranos*. Me and the other guys on the show use that to raise money for charities. We donate our time to various charities. People bid, in these auctions, for the pleasure of having lunch or dinner with us.

We have had people pay $30,000 just to have lunch with a bunch of us from the show. We've had people pay $25,000 to visit the set. One time a guy paid $50,000 to have about thirty of us come for lunch. It was Gandolfini and Michael Imperioli and Big Pussy and Artie Bucco and me and some more of the guys. He flew us in from all over the country, just for lunch. The money went to a cancer foundation. More recently, we donated our services to a cancer hospital in New Jersey. One of the guys from the show, his

Me, talking to the boss, as Joe Piscopo looks on.

father had been treated there. So we participated in the auction. I was the auctioneer. We were taking bids for lunch with the guys from the show. There were going to be twelve of us, having lunch at an Italian restaurant in New York.

The bidding was between two people. It got up to about $24,000. I suddenly said, "Is it worth $25,000? Then how about you pay $25,000 each, and we'll have lunch with *both* of you?"

They bought it. The hospital got two checks that night for $25,000 each.

The guys on the show do a lot of that. I organized a charity softball game that raised $80,000. A bunch of guys from the show came and participated. The ones that didn't come, some of them sent a check. Lots of people on the show donate autographed pictures of themselves to charities, to help them raise money. Almost every week, we'll pass around scripts and sign them, after we do read-throughs, and those will get donated to charities.

Sometimes it's kind of heavy. Eight of us recently went to Walter Reed Army Medical Center last winter. It was me and Aida Turturro and Lorraine Bracco and some of the other actors from the show. We took the train down to Washington. We took hats and DVDs, and we visited two different hospitals.

The wonderful Edie Falco, at our charity softball game.

And Lorraine Bracco.

It was great, and it was horrible. We met kids with their arms and legs blown off. We met a twenty-year-old kid who's missing two arms and one leg. Here's a kid who's lost his eyes. Here's a kid who'll never walk again. Here's a nineteen-year-old boy from Chicago who's in a coma. We met him, we met his family. We met wives and parents. We went to a rehab center where they're teaching kids to walk again.

Meeting us seemed to make them happy. But we went out that night and got smashed.

Sometimes, it's just fun. I was asked a couple of years ago to go down to New Orleans and be the grand marshal of their St. Joseph's parade. Not everyone knows this, but there are a lot of Italians in New Orleans—especially Sicilians. There was a time when New Orleans was known as "Little Palermo." In the 1800s, in fact, there were more Italians in New Orleans than anywhere else in America. That famous New Orleans sandwich, the muffuletta, that's pure Sicilian.

They take their heritage seriously, and they put on a huge

Tony Sirico, giving words of wisdom to Goomba Johnny.

parade every March 19—the saint day for Saint Joseph—as part of a celebration brought to Louisiana by the Sicilians. They get 100,000 locals to put on tuxedos and have a party, New Orleans goomba style.

My wife, Laura, and I were flown down, and picked up in a limo, and taken to a nice hotel. We were wined and dined like crazy by these great New Orleans goombas. They took us to Antoine's and Commander's Palace. We were treated like royalty.

Lots of famous Italians have been the grand marshal down there: Louis Prima. Rocky Marciano. Annette Funicello. James Darren, who's actually Italian and a friend of mine.

And then me. It was a huge honor to be asked. After the tragedy of Hurricane Katrina, I hope someday they'll hold that parade again, and that I can help celebrate.

So, when someone asks me to make a personal appearance for their little restaurant or their used car lot, and it's not someone who's a good friend, I ask them to make a donation to my kids' school or some other charity.

A guy asked me recently if I would show up at his wedding, because that would impress all his friends. What am I, Barney the dinosaur? Another guy asked me, "My fiancée is a big *Sopranos* fan. What would it cost to get you to come to my engagement party?" It's insulting. What's next, a nose and glasses?

The whole concept of the Goomba Diet is—go for it. Whatever you're doing, do it all the way. If you're in, you're all the way in. The Goomba Diet also says you should be grateful for what you've got and humble about how you got it.

There's some celebrities who could use the Goomba Diet. You know who I'm talking about. This one has it in her contract that she only washes her hair in Evian. This one's publicist tells everyone on the set you can't speak to him unless you're spoken to—or you're fired. This one has to have a bigger trailer than anyone else on the movie or he won't show up. For this one, the production has to employ a twenty-four-hour masseuse. For that one, the craft services people have to hire a twenty-four-hour macrobiotic chef.

I've seen some of the riders on their contracts. Even when they show up for a charity event, the caterers have to supply a certain kind of fruit, or a certain color of M&M, or a certain brand of beer.

When I was entertainment director at the Riviera, I had to listen to managers and agents dictate these things to me. I remember one actor, a guy with his own TV show, was coming up to do a couple of days. He had his agent call to tell the hotel to send someone to the airport to carry his bags. Get outta here! Carry his bags? He can carry his own bags!

When I travel, believe me, I carry my own bags. When I'm done working, I hail a cab. When I need something, I go buy it. I don't send somebody. I was looking for a shirt recently and this guy said to me, "You do your own shopping?" He was so impressed. Like, who the hell else is going to do my shopping? Who knows what I want more than me?

I think a lot of celebrities get the wrong idea about how to act from watching the way other celebrities before them have acted. Maybe they think you have to act like a big star in order to be famous, or stay famous, or something. They think you have to be a jerk to get what you want.

I don't think so. The rules for famous people are the rules for everyone else. They're very simple.

BEING FAMOUS ON THE GOOMBA DIET

- Do be polite.
- Do tip.
- Don't pinch the waitress's ass.
- Remember to enjoy it. Because it's not going to last.

Some guys I know take advantage, right from the start. They want the freebies. They want the handouts. If they show up anyplace, they expect to be paid.

I know an actor who sits in the same little café every single day and charges people $20 to take his picture. I know another actor who was in an antique store trying to buy something that cost $40. He told the guy, "What if I pay you twenty and send you an autographed picture?" The guy said that was okay. Then the actor never sent him the picture.

That's got to take a little something out of you every time you do it.

Other actors spend weeks out of the year going to conventions and comic book shows. If you ever go to one, I guarantee you'll see people like Carrie Fisher from *Star Wars* and Butch Patrick from *The Munsters* there. I know, because I've been. They pay you $5,000 to sign five hundred pictures, say, before the event starts. Then you get people coming by your booth paying you $20 to sign something of theirs—a photo, a magazine article, whatever.

This would be great, I guess, except if the guy in the booth next to you turns out to be Captain Kirk or something. He gets all the action and you feel like an idiot. You go home depressed because you got beat by one of the kids from *The Brady Bunch*.

I'm not knocking it. A man's got to pay the rent somehow. It's just not for me—or not yet, anyway. Maybe twenty years from now I'll feel lucky to get the booth next to Mary Ann from *Gilligan's Island*.

All this stuff could make you bitter. It could make you angry. You could start to mistreat people.

That's because you're *too* famous. You have too much celebrity. It went to your head. If that happens, watch out. Here are some warning signs:

YOU KNOW YOU'RE TOO FAMOUS WHEN . . .

- You have your own fragrance, and it smells better than you ever did.
- Your picture is on the front page of the paper, and you're not even in handcuffs.
- More people recognize you from magazine covers than from the wall at the post office.
- You get asked to put your feet in wet cement—and you don't have to leave them there.
- Paris Hilton asks for *your* autograph.

I don't kid myself. I don't think I got all these breaks because I deserve it. A lot of it is luck and timing. The stars in the sky have to be lined up. I know, when I go in for an audition, that I might not get the job. It could be I'm too fat, or I'm too skinny, or I'm too tall, or I'm too old, or I'm not old enough. A lot of what happens in life is just being in the right place at the right time—and being ready to do something about it. I absolutely know I could still be a maître d' in Las Vegas, doing exactly what I was doing ten years ago, with no future as an actor at all.

And that would be fine.

In the end, the upside of having a career and being a little famous outweighs the downside completely. I get invited places I would never get invited. I get to help people I'd never have the opportunity to help. I get to show my kids things they'd never see.

I'm famous enough already. The other day I got stopped by a lady who wanted my autograph. She had three teeth and worked at Starbucks. Any more famous than that, I couldn't handle it.

On the other hand, getting to be a little famous, and doing what I've been doing to get there, has been the greatest. Remember, I'm just a fat goomba from Brooklyn. It wasn't that long ago I was standing on the street corner wondering what I was going to do with my life. Now, I'm on friendly terms with Jay Leno, and I'm doing these bits for *The Tonight Show*. I'm interviewing John Kerry! I'm covering the Boston Marathon. I'm flying down to Georgia to cover the Redneck Games. Okay, that's not so glamorous, but I got paid to do it—to go someplace and see some things I would never get the chance to see otherwise.

I've been part of the most critically acclaimed show on television. I've gotten the opportunity to work with incredibly talented people—like the show's creator, David Chase—and I've been able to become friends with all of the cast.

I've been invited to fancy houses and served fancy dinners. I've been to the most expensive restaurants in New York, Chicago, Los Angeles, Las Vegas—you name it. I've stayed in the best hotels in the country.

When I go, I go first class. And being part of *The Sopranos* and *The Tonight Show* and all the films I've worked on has made that possible.

So I'm grateful. And I think the best way I can show my gratitude is to just continue to do what I'm doing, to be the guy I am—sticking to the Goomba Diet, and making the world a little more goomba, one neighborhood at a time.